MW00747972

brilliant
barbecues

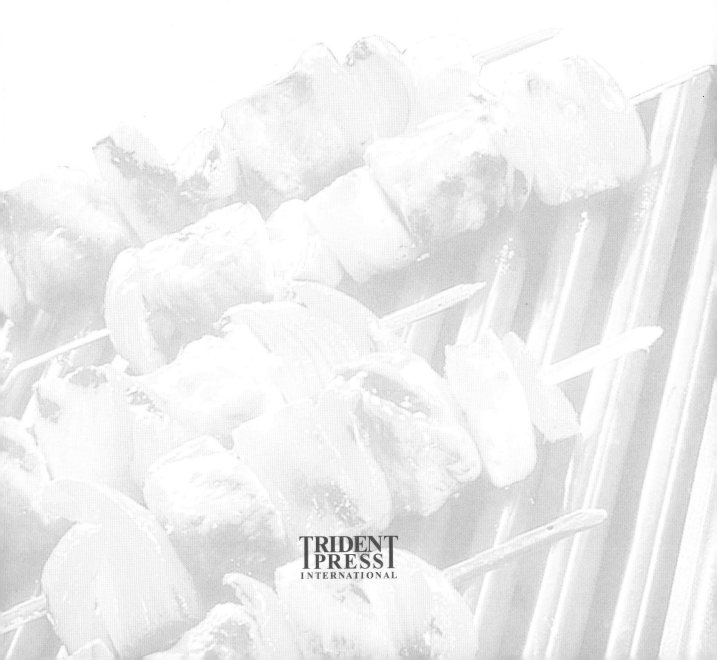

TRIDENT
PRESS
INTERNATIONAL

Published by:
TRIDENT PRESS INTERNATIONAL
801, 12th Avenue South
Suite 302
Naples, FL 34102 U.S.A.
Copyright (c)Trident Press International 2001
Tel: (941) 649 7077
Fax: (941) 649 5832
Email: tridentpress@worldnet.att.net
Website: www.trident-international.com

acknowledgements

Brilliant Barbecues

Designed & Compiled by: R&R Publications Marketing Pty. Ltd.
Creative Director: Paul Sims
Production Manager: Anthony Carroll
Food Photography: Warren Webb, William Meppem, Andrew Elton, Quentin Bacon, Gary Smith, Per Ericson, Paul Grater, Ray Joice, John Stewart, Ashley Mackevicius, Harm Mol, Yanto Noerianto, Andy Payne.
Food Stylists: Stephane Souvlis, Janet Lodge, Di Kirby, Wendy Berecry, Belinda Clayton, Rosemary De Santis, Carolyn Fienberg, Jacqui Hing, Michelle Gorry, Christine Sheppard, Donna Hay.
Recipe Development: Ellen Argyriou, Sheryle Eastwood, Kim Freeman, Lucy Kelly, Donna Hay, Anneka Mitchell, Penelope Peel, Jody Vassallo, Belinda Warn, Loukie Werle.
Proof Reader: Andrea Tarttelin

All rights reserved. No part of this book may be stored, reproduced or transmitted in any form or by any means without written permission of the publisher, except in the case of brief quotations embodied in critical articles and reviews.

Includes Index
ISBN 1 58279 093 0
EAN 9 781582 790930

First Edition Printed June 2001
Computer Typeset in Humanist 521 & Times New Roman

Printed in Hong Kong

Which barbecue?

There are many different barbecues available. The one you choose will depend on your budget, how many people you regularly feed and whether barbecuing is usually a planned or an impromptu affair.

Gas barbecues:

These barbecues contain lava rocks which are heated by gas burners. The lava rocks evenly distribute the heat and if you have a barbecue with multiple burners it is possible to have the rocks hot on one side and a medium heat on the other. The rack on which you cook the food is set above the rocks. Gas barbecues also require a gas bottle, which needs to be refilled on a regular basis – this is relatively inexpensive. When lighting a gas barbecue it is important to follow the manufacturer's instructions. If the barbecue does not ignite immediately, turn it off, wait for any build up of gas to disperse, then try again.

Wood or coal barbecues:

The key to using these types of barbecues is patience and planning. These barbecues take up to an hour to heat, so you need to remember to light the barbecue well in advance.

Electric barbecues:

These are ideal for people who want to barbecue indoors and, like gas barbecues, they produce almost instant heat.

How hot?

The recipes in this book were cooked on a gas barbecue. Gas barbecues heat up very quickly and the heat is relatively easy to control, however if your barbecue uses coal, wood or barbecue fuel, you need to allow
30-45 minutes for coals to heat and 45 minutes to 1 hour for wood. The following is a guide for assessing the heat of these barbecues.

Hot fire:

There will be a red glow showing through the thin layer of white ash and when you hold your hand 15 cm/6 in above the coals you will only be able to leave it there for 3 seconds. This fire is ideal for searing and quick cooking.

Medium fire:

The red glow will be almost gone and the ash thicker and more grey in colour. When you hold your hand 15 cm/6 in above the coals you will be able to leave it there for 5-7 seconds. Most barbecuing is done on this heat.

This summer, Lowe's brings the indoors outdoors by introducing two exclusive Jenn-Air grills. Jenn-Air appliances have always been among the top-rated by consumers, and since the introduction of the first self-ventilated cooktop and oven more than forty years ago, Jenn-Air has a reputation as a leader in technology. The Jenn-Air grills are no exception. They include lids and sear plates made out of porcelain and stainless steel, electronic ignition and either four or five stainless steel tube burners with individual controls. Not only is Lowe's the first to sell Jenn-Air grills outside of specialty stores, Lowe's carries other great brands like Charbroil and Weber. Lowe's has got the grill for your backyard paradise. With more than 740 stores in 42 states, Lowe's is one of the nation's leaders in home improvement and home decor. Lowe's offers in-store kitchen design, complete installation services, and weekly how-to-clinics for the do-it-yourselfer. For more information, visit **www.Lowes.com.**

GRILL CRAZY

Long gone are the days when a backyard barbecue meant simply beans and franks—and the attendant scavenging mosquitoes. The backyard has become a respite from the rest of the world. From furniture to foliage to pest control, people are creating sanctuaries for relaxing and entertaining. That includes cooking and meal preparation. As the kitchen has become the center of the home, the grill has become a centerpiece of outdoor entertaining. There's a new grill in town, with amazing features and attractive designs that give cooking enthusiasts more reasons than ever to beef up their outdoor kitchens this summer. The modern grill has features like electronic ignition systems, which light faster and more consistently. Cooking grids of porcelain cast iron distribute heat more evenly and sear meats and vegetables beautifully—not to mention they don't rust and they're easier to clean.

Improving Home Improvement

©2002 Sutter Home Winery, Inc., St. Helena, CA

BUILD A BETTER BURGER®
and WIN $20,000

Presented by The American Culinary Federation

To enter the 2002 grilled burger recipe contest,
visit www.buildabetterburger.com

Ten finalists and their guests will be flown to the Napa Valley for the annual
Build A Better Burger® Cook-off on Saturday, September 28, 2002.
(Roundtrip airfare and hotel accommodations included.)

★ $20,000 will be awarded for the best beef or veal burger.
★ $10,000 will be awarded for the best alternative burger.
★ $5,000 will be awarded for the "People's Choice" award.

Join us in the fun!

Sponsored by: SUTTER HOME® Winery  BEEF IT'S WHAT'S FOR DINNER®

Into the Woods

Wood chips, chunks, and planks add an irresistible smoky taste to grilled foods of all kinds

BY DORIE GREENSPAN

A FEW YEARS AGO, a Parisian friend of mine, a trendsetter in just about every possible way, asked if I'd bring her a charcoal grill. With it she would be the first on her block to possess what was to become, just a short time later, the hottest must-have item in the City of Light.

The way she described it, I assumed she wanted one of those portable grills you tote to the beach, and I was delighted that I could be a good friend without buying a companion ticket for an oversize kettle drum with legs. Wrong. Of course, she wanted the biggest grill available, and it had to be black—even a grill must be chic. That's how my husband and I found ourselves stopped by the customs man, who suspected we were trafficking in computers (don't ask). It's also how I came to have an inexhaustible supply of gift ideas for my *amie*. Once you have a grill, you can go as accessory-crazy as if you'd bought the perfect little black dress.

I've bought her great grilling gear, but this year I have an *ooh-la-la* idea—wood chips and planks. *Sans doute,* she'll love the flavors she'll get from them and, since chips and planks are still a little esoteric in the States, she's bound to get a kick out of being first with the latest—again.

Wood chips—and chunks—are the stuff of smoke and smoky flavors. In log form, they were once solely the domain of serious pit barbecuers and smokers. Now they're widely available, come in a dizzying number of woods (and therefore flavors), and can be used to smoke, grill, and barbecue on just about any backyard grill.

Chunks, which can also be used as you would use charcoal, and chips can be purchased in woods that are traditional for smoking—oak, hickory, maple, pecan, alder, and mesquite—as well as in the more *recherché* apple, peach, and sassafras.

If you've never used these flavor builders, you should read your grill's manual for the how-tos or consult Steven Raichlen's book *The Barbecue! Bible.* But here's what you need to know: Whether you're using chips or chunks, you must use hardwoods. No throwing your old pine paneling into the fire—soft woods burn too quickly and have resins that will ruin your food. In addition, both chips and chunks need to be thoroughly soaked (in water or even cider or beer) and drained before they are put onto the fire—remember, you want smoke, not flames. And while you can just toss the wood over your coals or lava rocks, cleanup is easier if you use your grill's smoker drawer (if there is one), enclose the wood in a perforated foil pouch, or put it in a smoke box, a cast-iron box with a slotted top. (I hope my Parisian friend isn't reading this—I'd rather not carry cast iron across the Atlantic!)

To find this gear, try your local hardware store or go to naturesownonline.com. (Nature's Own is a good nationally available brand for chips, chunks, and a smoke box.) And if you get hooked on smoke, remember that you can use fresh herbs and grapevines the same way you use wood chips.

For a different way to get a woody flavor, try the centuries-old technique of cooking food on a plank. This is a method practiced by Native Americans from the Pacific Northwest, who most commonly cook salmon (though bluefish and other oily fish work well, too) on cedar or alder planks over open fires. Planking is probably the easiest, cleanest way to give food a lightly smoky flavor, since you have nothing to do but plop the plank (really just a board) on the grill and plop the fish on the plank. Best of all, when grilling season ends, you can go ahead and use the plank in your oven. You can buy thick cedar planks that will be good for about a lifetime (small ones are $40; big ones, $50) at plankcooking.com or, from the same source, six thin use-'em-then-toss-'em planks that should be soaked before using (called Barbecue Grilling Planks; $16 for the pack).

Maybe I *should* drag this stuff to Paris. After all, I might get some apple-smoked foie gras in exchange. Sounds like a good deal, *n'est-ce pas?*

PHOTOGRAPHY BY RICK SZCZECHOWSKI

Martha Living Omnimedia, Inc. All Rights Reserved.

table
talk

MARTHA STEWART everyday®

From left to right: Balustrade Double Old-Fashioneds, Set of 4; Cottage Stainless-Steel Flatware 20-Piece Set, shown in Ivory; Salad/Dinner Plate and Soup Bowls, from Acorn-Embossed 20-Piece Dinnerware Set.

With Martha Stewart Everyday™ dinnerware, flatware, beverageware, and napkins, you have all you need to set your table in style. Get to Kmart and get set.

Available exclusively at Kmart, kmart.com, and through marthastewart.com

Hoisin Around

Salty and smoky, sweet and savory, this Chinese sauce adds a whole new dimension to summer foods—including barbecue

TEXT BY LESLEE KOMAIKO
RECIPES BY VICTORIA ABBOTT RICCARDI

CUCUMBER AND WATERMELON SALAD WITH HOISIN-LIME DRESSING

A Vietnamese-style salad that makes a refreshing accompaniment to any kind of barbecued meat.

6 SERVINGS

1½ large English hothouse cucumbers, cut into ½-inch pieces (about 3 cups)
3 cups ½-inch cubes seeded watermelon

3½ tablespoons fresh lime juice
3 tablespoons hoisin sauce
¼ cup chopped fresh cilantro
2 tablespoons chopped fresh mint
⅓ cup coarsely chopped lightly salted dry-roasted peanuts

Combine cucumbers and watermelon in medium bowl. Cover with plastic wrap and refrigerate at least 15 minutes and up to 4 hours. Drain; discard liquid.

Whisk lime juice and hoisin sauce in small bowl to blend. Pour dressing over cucumber-watermelon mixture and toss gently. Season salad to taste with pepper. Sprinkle salad with cilantro, mint, and then peanuts. Serve immediately.

I AM NOT the biggest fan of condiments, especially bottled condiments. Most are one-note affairs with little complexity. I'll take a drizzle of ketchup, maybe a smidgen of mayo, a dash of soy, but that's about it. Unless we're talking about hoisin.

Hoisin sauce, also known as Peking sauce, is a Chinese table condiment that is at once sweet, spicy, salty, smoky, and robust. And when heated, it has a deep earthy aroma.

I love the stuff.

In this, I am not alone. Americans, it seems, like hoisin even more than the Chinese do. Maybe it's the sugar, or maybe it's the salt. In either case, at Chinese restaurants across the country, diners like me can be spotted spooning extra hoisin onto our *mushu* pork pancakes and Peking duck.

And now that grilling season is well under way, it's worth noting that hoisin is particularly well suited to barbecue. In Canton, China, where the sauce originated hundreds of years ago, two of the most celebrated dishes are barbecue preparations ➤

PHOTOGRAPHY BY DAVID PRINCE

your PalmPilot to confirm which city you're in.

"Blue Smoke is ninety-nine percent soul and one percent head," says Meyer. No wanton "creativity" here. This means brine-curing chicken, putting ham hocks in the split pea soup, baking white bread with buttermilk. Everything is treated with the same respectful touch. And the results are devastatingly good.

Gyu-Kaku
LOS ANGELES

After opening more than four hundred Korean barbecue restaurants in Japan, the Gyu-Kaku (*goo-KAH-ku*) chain has sprouted an outpost in Los Angeles, where waiting patrons spill out onto the sidewalk every night.

Unlike in the United States, grilling is anything but a backyard event in Japan and Korea. Gyu-Kaku executive Kunao Kim says that when people want grilled food in those countries, they go to restaurants, where the experience is as communal as it is gustatory. "People sitting around the grill sharing food develop a special relationship," she says.

Gyu-Kaku grills in the *yakiniku* style, which tweaks the Korean barbecue formula, offering portions more dainty in size (about four ounces) than at the typical Korean protein palace. You can graze through two to five grill orders at $5 or $6 each. As at all Korean barbecue restaurants, you cook the meat yourself, but here you get to choose from several marinade possibilities.

Some of my favorite selections on a recent visit were the boneless short rib with *shiso* marinade, thin slices of bone-in short rib with a rich, *mirin*-based *ta're* marinade, flavorful skirt steak slices, and wonderful *kurobuta* pork sausages.

Costa's
CHICAGO

For years, restaurants in Greektown have offered menu staples from the grill—usually lots of lamb and skewered meat. About seven years ago, however, neighborhood restaurateur Costa Vlahos introduced a wider range of grilled dishes at Costa's—some of them lighter, with more

DO-IT-YOURSELF KOREAN BARBECUE AT GYU-KAKU IN LOS ANGELES.

seafood and vegetables added to the mix.

Appetizers show off this new Greek grilling most resoundingly. I particularly like the roasted stuffed Florini peppers, dark-red peppers stuffed with a tangy combination of feta and *graviera* cheeses, scorched on the grill, then drizzled with balsamic vinegar. They are an intense, eye-opening blast of the Mediterranean. You'll want to stay for the main courses, such as double-cut grilled lamb chops and a fabulous center-cut filet mignon swimming in herb-inflected juices.

Vlahos recently sold the restaurant but stayed on as manager, making sure everything is just so. "For most people in Greece, grilling is an everyday event," he says. "They think the food just tastes better." And if they're cooking it like they do at Costa's, they're right.

Fogo de Chão
DALLAS

Another grill cuisine sweeping the country right now is Brazilian barbecue. *Churrascarias* in Brazil are restaurants that provide an all-you-can-eat binge for carnivores. Cooking is done "*rodízio*-style," meaning that waiters (often dressed as gauchos) turn huge skewers of meat over an open flame, then bring these meaty swords to your table.

For several years *churrascarias* have been going full force in New York, Miami, Las Vegas, and—most fittingly—the great beef-eating state of Texas. That's where a small Brazilian restaurant chain called

Fogo de Chão opened its first U.S. restaurant in Dallas in 1997 (branches have since appeared in Houston, Atlanta, and Chicago).

At Fogo de Chão, there are fifteen different cuts of meat that will pass your way. As at most *churrascarias*, the *picanha*, or rump steak, is delicious. Also terrific are the *alcatra* (top sirloin), the *fraldinha* (bottom sirloin), and the *lombo* (pork loin).

The Helmand
BALTIMORE

Middle Eastern barbecue, in the form of grilled kebabs and *schwarma* and the like, has in the past failed to generate much excitement. But The Helmand could change that, thanks to two brothers, Abdul Qayum and Mahmood Karzai, the older brothers of Afghanistan's interim prime minister, Hamid Karzai. They run a trio of restaurants in Baltimore; Cambridge, Massachusetts; and San Francisco.

The first of these restaurants—each named The Helmand, after a river in southern Afghanistan—opened in Baltimore in 1989. It's a busy spot decorated with Afghan arts and crafts. Afghan cooking lies somewhere between the Persian idea of grilling and the Indian-Pakistani notion of spicing, though it's more gently spiced. Many of the grilled meats are marinated with just a few ingredients in exquisite balance—coriander, garlic, yogurt—which leads to an amazing flavor.

Most distinctively Afghan are dried grapes, wildly tart. I tasted them in a superb special called *chopan*—a grilled rack of lamb. The grapes also lend spark to the *seekh* kebab, made from lamb chunks, and to the *chopendez,* an excellent beef kebab. A great light choice is the *mourgh* and *mahi* kebab—marinated chunks of chicken breast alternated on the skewer with marinated chunks of fresh tuna.

Is it barbecue? Is it grill food? I dunno. Let's leave that to the lexicographers. For the rest of us: Let's get it while it's hot. ◀

David Rosengarten is publisher and editor-in-chief of The Rosengarten Report, *a newsletter about food, wine, and travel.*

FRAN GEALER

AN ELEGANT SURPRISE: HEARTS OF ROMAINE TOPPED WITH TOASTED PECANS AND ROQUEFORT DRESSING (RECIPE ON PAGE 42).

onions and sauté until soft and starting to brown, about 10 minutes. Add balsamic vinegar. Sprinkle with salt and pepper. Simmer until onions are deep brown, stirring occasionally, about 10 minutes. Remove from heat. (*Can be prepared 1 hour ahead. Let stand at room temperature. Wrap in foil and reheat on grill 10 minutes before serving.*)

Grill burgers until cooked through, about 5 minutes per side. Place 1 burger on bottom half of each bun. Top with onions and bun tops and serve.

GRILLED CORN ON THE COB WITH CHIPOTLE BUTTER

This recipe has a nice balance of sweet and spicy flavors, and a drizzle of lime juice provides tang. Serve the corn and the romaine salad (see recipe) with the burgers, and check out the box on the next page for potato salad suggestions.

8 SERVINGS

½ cup (1 stick) unsalted
    butter
1½ tablespoons minced seeded
    canned chipotle chilies*
2 teaspoons fresh lime
    juice
¼ teaspoon salt

8 large ears of corn, husked

Lime wedges

Melt butter in small saucepan over medium heat. Add minced chipotles, fresh lime juice, and ¼ teaspoon salt. Reduce heat to low and cook chipotle butter 1 minute to blend flavors.

Place ears of corn on baking sheet. Brush corn all over with chipotle butter. (*Can be prepared 4 hours ahead. Cover corn and refrigerate.*)

Prepare barbecue (medium-high heat). Grill corn until cooked through and blackened in spots, turning frequently, about 6 minutes. Serve corn with lime wedges.

*Chipotle chilies canned in a spicy tomato sauce, sometimes called adobo, *are available at Latin American markets, specialty foods stores, and some supermarkets.* ➤

SUN-DRIED-TOMATO BURGERS WITH BALSAMIC-GLAZED ONIONS

A mixture of ground sirloin and ground chuck works best for these. (Don't use lean or extra-lean meat—the burgers won't be nearly as juicy.) Cold beer is the perfect accompaniment, so put bottles of Indian pale ale on ice; for guests who prefer wine, pour a fruity Beaujolais.

8 SERVINGS

3 pounds ground beef
1⅓ cups chopped drained sun-dried
    tomatoes packed in oil,
    6 tablespoons oil reserved
½ cup grated onion
3 tablespoons dried basil
2 teaspoons ground cumin
½ teaspoon salt
¼ teaspoon ground black pepper

3 onions, halved, thinly
    sliced
¼ cup balsamic vinegar

8 hamburger buns, toasted

Line large baking sheet with parchment paper. Mix ground beef, chopped sun-dried tomatoes, 2 tablespoons reserved tomato oil, grated onion, dried basil, ground cumin, ½ teaspoon salt, and ¼ teaspoon pepper in large bowl. Form mixture into 8 patties. Transfer patties to prepared baking sheet. Cover with plastic wrap and refrigerate at least 1 hour. (*Can be prepared 4 hours ahead. Keep chilled.*)

Prepare barbecue (medium-high heat). Heat remaining 4 tablespoons reserved tomato oil in heavy large skillet over medium-high heat. Add sliced

MODERN MARVEL?

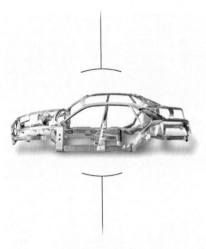

MODERN ART?

Aluminum. It's virtually impossible to work with. But we knew that if we could create a viable aluminum frame it would result in a car that would be lighter, stronger and safer than its steel competitors. In short, a technological marvel. Forty patents and more than 10 years later, we crafted a premium luxury sedan with the revolutionary all-aluminum Audi Space Frame. Partnered with quattro® all-wheel drive, the A8 became legendary. But we didn't stop there. With a roaring 360 hp engine and a sportier suspension, the S8 continues to set standards in its class.

Never quit. Never do the expected. Never rest on your laurels. Never think great is good enough. NEVER FOLLOW.™

audiusa.com See your dealer or call 1-800-FOR-AUDI for information regarding performance tires. "Audi," "quattro," "A8" and the four rings emblem are registered trademarks and "S8" and "Never Follow" are trademarks of AUDI AG. ©2002 Audi of America, Inc.

which
barbecue

Low *fire*:

The red glow will have disappeared and there will be a thick coating of grey ash. This heat is ideal for slow cooking of foods.

The amount of heat reaching the food on these barbecues can also be controlled by moving the rack closer to or further away from the fire.

If you have a wood barbecue, interesting flavours can be imparted to the food by using different types of wood. It is well to be aware that there are some plants that are poisonous and wood from those plants or chemically treated timber, is not suitable for barbecuing. Depending on where you live some of the following may be available: fruit woods, such as cherry and apple, which give a mild sweet flavour that is delicious when cooking pork, poultry and fish; grapevine cuttings – these give a delicate sweet flavour that is excellent for fish and poultry. Herbs such as rosemary and thyme also give interesting flavours when burned on the barbecue.

which
barbecue

Play it safe

As with any type of cooking, basic safety rules should always be observed. However with barbecuing there are a few extra that you need to remember.

- If you have a gas barbecue, before lighting it check that all the gas fittings and hose connections are tight.
- If your gas barbecue does not light first time, turn it off, wait 20 seconds and try again. This will ensure that there is no gas build-up.
- Always turn a gas barbecue off at the gas bottle as well as at the controls.
- Check the barbecue area before lighting the barbecue. Do not have the barbecue too close to the house and sweep up any dry leaves or anything that might catch fire if hit by a spark.
- Watch a lighted barbecue at all times. Keep children and pets away from hot barbecues and equipment.
- Do not barbecue in enclosed areas. If wet weather has forced you to move your barbecue undercover, ensure there is plenty of ventilation.
- Remember always to check the manufacturer's safety instructions that come with your barbecue.

Equipment check

Use this checklist to ensure that you have the basic equipment for successful barbecuing.

oven mitt or cloth – important for handling hot skewers, racks and frying pans.

tongs – these should be long-handled so that you can turn food without burning your hands. Use tongs for turning food, testing to see if steak is done and moving coals and hot racks.

basting brushes – these are used to brush food with marinades, oil, butter or sauce during cooking.

spatulas – essential for turning delicate foods, such as fish, so that they do not fall apart. The best type has a long, wide blade and a long handle.

selection of sharp knives – use for preparation and carving cooked food.

hinged grills, wire baskets – these come in many shapes and sizes for cooking whole fish and other foods that are difficult to turn. Always oil the grill or basket before using so that the food does not stick.

skewers – bamboo or wooden skewers are good for quick cooking of foods. Before use, soak them in water to prevent them from burning during cooking. Before threading food onto bamboo or wooden skewers, lightly oil them so that the cooked food will slip off easily. Metal skewers are better for heavier foods.

marinating pans and bowls – remember that most marinades contain an acid ingredient so the best choice of dish for marinating is glass, ceramic, stainless steel or enamel. Deep-sided disposable aluminium dishes are also good for marinating.

Middle Eastern dip

appetise

Whilst the barbecue is warming up

and to put your guests into a casual mood, serve a selection of off-barbecue appetisers with drinks. These tasty morsels will really get things going.

middle
eastern dip

Photograph page 9

ingredients

1 large eggplant (aubergine)
1 onion, unpeeled
2 cloves garlic, crushed
olive oil
2 tablespoons lemon juice
2 tablespoons chopped fresh parsley
¹/₄ cup/60g/2oz sour cream
4 pieces lavash bread, cut into triangles

Method:

1 Preheat barbecue to a high heat. Place eggplant (aubergine) and onion on lightly oiled barbecue grill and cook, turning occasionally, for 20-30 minutes or until skins of eggplant (aubergine) and onion are charred and flesh is soft. Cool slightly, peel and chop roughly.

2 Place eggplant (aubergine), onion, garlic, ¹/₄ cup/60mL/2fl oz oil and lemon juice in a food processor or blender and process until smooth. Add parsley and sour cream and mix to combine.

3 Brush bread lightly with oil and cook on barbecue for 1-2 minutes each side or until crisp. Serve immediately with dip.
Lavash bread is a yeast-free Middle Eastern bread available from Middle Eastern food shops and some supermarkets. If unavailable use pitta bread instead.

Serves 6

spicy
barbecued nuts

ingredients

250g/8oz honey roasted peanuts
185g/6oz pecans
125g/4 oz macadamia nuts
125g/4oz cashews
1 tablespoon sweet paprika
1 tablespoon ground cumin
2 teaspoons garam masala
1 teaspoon ground coriander
1 teaspoon ground nutmeg
¹/₄ teaspoon cayenne pepper or according to taste
1 tablespoon olive oil

Method:

1 Preheat barbecue to a medium heat. Place peanuts, pecans, macadamia nuts and cashews in a bowl and mix to combine. Add paprika, cumin, garam masala, coriander, nutmeg and cayenne pepper and toss to coat.

2 Heat oil on barbecue plate (griddle), add nut mixture and cook, turning frequently, for 5 minutes or until nuts are golden. Cool slightly before serving.
Warning: the nuts are very hot when first removed from the barbecue and they retain their heat for quite a long time - so caution your guests when you serve these delicious nibbles.

Serves 6

Oven temperature 180°C, 350°F, Gas 4

smoked
salmon and watercress roulade

Method:

1 Place watercress leaves, parsley, egg yolks, flour and pepper to taste in a food processor and process until mixture is smooth. Transfer watercress mixture to a bowl. Place egg whites in a bowl and beat until stiff peaks form. Fold egg white mixture into watercress mixture.

2 Spoon roulade mixture into a greased and lined 26x32cm/10¹/₂x12³/₄ in Swiss roll tin and bake for 5 minutes or until just cooked. Turn roulade onto a damp teatowel and roll up from short side. Set aside to cool.

3 To make filling, place cream cheese, sour cream, smoked salmon and lemon juice in a food processor and process until mixture is smooth. Stir gelatine mixture into smoked salmon mixture.

4 Unroll cold roulade, spread with filling and reroll. Cover and chill. Cut into slices to serve.

Serves 10

ingredients

1 bunch/90g/3oz watercress
1 teaspoon finely chopped fresh parsley
2 eggs, separated
2 tablespoons flour
freshly ground black pepper

<u>**Smoked salmon filling**</u>
60g/2oz cream cheese
2 tablespoons sour cream
90g/3oz smoked salmon
1 teaspoon lemon juice
1¹/₂ teaspoons gelatine dissolved in
1¹/₂ tablespoons hot water, cooled

fruit
and cheese platter

Photograph page 13

Method:
1 Place lemon juice in a small bowl, add red and green apple wedges and toss to coat. This will help prevent the apple wedges from going brown.
2 Arrange red and green apple wedges, kiwifruit slices, orange segments, Camembert, Stilton and tasty (mature cheddar) cheeses attractively with biscuits and dip on a large platter.
Note: Choose fruit in season and arrange with your favourite cheeses on a large platter.
Serves 10

ingredients

3 tablespoons fresh lemon juice
2 red-skinned apples, cored and cut into wedges
2 green-skinned apples, cored and cut into wedges
4 kiwifruit, peeled and cut into slices
2 oranges, peeled, segmented and white pith removed
100g/4oz Camembert cheese
100g/4oz Stilton cheese
100g/4oz tasty cheese (mature cheddar), choose your favourite brand
cheese biscuits, purchased or homemade

passion fruit
yoghurt dip

Photograph page 13

Method:
1 Place yogurt, honey and passion fruit pulp in a bowl and mix to combine.
The perfect accompaniment to any fresh fruit.
Makes 2 cups/400g/12¹/₂oz

ingredients

2 cups/400 g/12¹/₂oz unsweetened natural yogurt
2 tablespoons honey
3 tablespoons passion fruit pulp or pulp 4-5 passion fruit

guacamole
with tortillas

Photograph page 15

Method:
1 To make Chilli Butter, place butter, lemon rind, chilli sauce and cumin in a bowl and mix to combine.
2 To make Guacamole, place avocado in a bowl and mash with a fork. Stir in tomato, lemon juice and coriander or parsley.
3 Place tortillas in a single layer on a baking tray and heat on barbecue for 3-5 minutes or until warm.
   To serve: Place Chilli Butter, Guacamole and tortillas on a platter so that each person can spread a tortilla with Chilli Butter, top with Guacamole, then roll up and eat.
Serves 6

ingredients

6 corn tortillas

Chilli butter
90g/3oz butter
2 teaspoons finely grated lemon rind
2 teaspoons sweet chilli sauce
1 teaspoon ground cumin

Guacamole
1 avocado, halved, stoned and peeled
1 tomato, peeled and finely chopped
2 tablespoons lemon juice
1 tablespoon finely chopped fresh coriander or parsley

cheese
and bacon nachos

Photograph page 15

Method:
1 Cook bacon, spring onions and chillies in a nonstick frying pan over a medium heat for 4-5 minutes or until crisp. Remove from pan and drain on absorbent kitchen paper.
2 Place corn chips in a shallow oven-proof dish and sprinkle with bacon mixture and cheese. Bake for 5-8 minutes or until heated through and cheese is melted. Serve immediately, accompanied with sour cream for dipping.
   Jalapeño chillies: These are the medium-to-dark green chillies that taper to a blunt end and are 5-7 $\frac{1}{2}$ cm/2-3 in long and 2-2 $\frac{1}{2}$ cm/ $\frac{3}{4}$-1 in wide. They are medium-to-hot in taste and are also available canned or bottled.
Serves 6

ingredients

6 rashers bacon, finely chopped
6 spring onions, finely chopped
4 jalapeño chillies, finely chopped
200g/6 $\frac{1}{2}$oz packet corn chips
125g/4oz grated tasty cheese (mature cheddar)
1 cup/250g/8oz sour cream

grilled cod and potatoes

sizzling
seafood

With their cooking times fish and

seafood are perfect for barbecuing. This imaginative

selection of dishes will have you serving these water

creatures from the barbecue regularly.

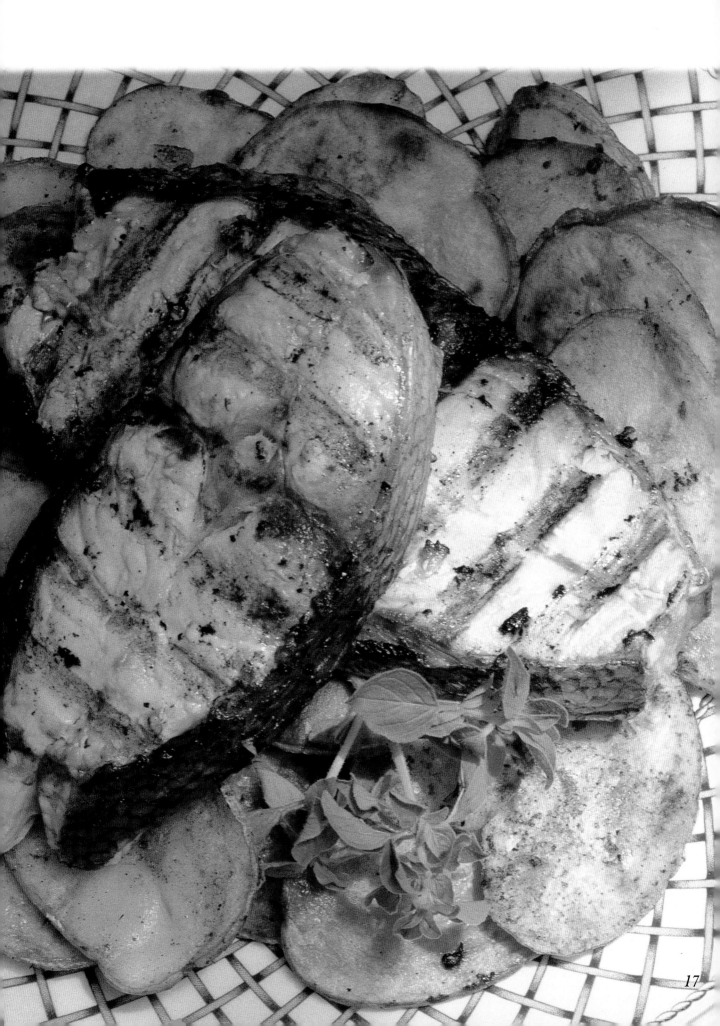

whole fish
in banana leaves

Method:

1 Preheat barbecue to a medium heat. Blanch banana leaf in boiling water for 1 minute, drain, pat dry and set aside.

2 To make stuffing, place rice, pistachio nuts, sun-dried peppers or tomatoes, spring onions, dill, lemon rind and garlic in a bowl and mix to combine. Spoon stuffing into cavity of fish and secure opening with wooden toothpicks or cocktail sticks.

3 Place fish in centre of banana leaf, top with lime slices and dill and fold banana leaf around fish to completely enclose. Secure with wooden toothpicks or cocktail sticks. Alternately wrap fish in lightly oiled aluminium foil.

4 Place fish on barbecue grill and cook for 7-10 minutes, turn and cook for 7-10 minutes longer or until flesh flakes when tested with a fork.

Serves 4

ingredients

1 large banana leaf
1 large whole fish such as sea bass or snapper, cleaned and skin scored at 3cm/1¼in intervals
1 lime, thinly sliced
4 sprigs fresh dill

Nutty rice stuffing
1 cup/220g/7oz wild rice blend, cooked
90g/3oz pistachio nuts, chopped
3 tablespoons finely chopped sun-dried peppers or tomatoes
3 spring onions, chopped
1 tablespoon chopped fresh dill
1 teaspoon finely grated lemon rind
1 clove garlic, chopped

grilled
cod and potatoes

Photograph page 17

Method:

1 Preheat barbecue to a medium heat. Place 1 tablespoon oil, lime juice and black peppercorns in a bowl and mix to combine. Brush oil mixture over fish and marinate at room temperature for 10 minutes.

2 Brush potatoes with oil and sprinkle with salt. Place potatoes on lightly oiled barbecue grill and cook for 5 minutes each side or until tender and golden. Move potatoes to side of barbecue to keep warm.

3 Place fish on lightly oiled barbecue grill and cook for 3-5 minutes each side or until flesh flakes when tested with a fork. To serve, arrange potatoes attractively on serving plates and top with fish.

Serves

ingredients

3 tablespoons olive oil
2 tablespoons lime juice
1 teaspoon crushed black peppercorns
4 cod cutlets
6 potatoes, very thinly sliced
sea salt

hot
chilli prawns (shrimp)

Method:

1 To make marinade, place black pepper, chilli sauce, soy sauce, garlic and lemon juice in a bowl and mix to combine. Add prawns (shrimp), toss to coat, cover and set aside to marinate for 1 hour. Toss several times during marinating.

2 To make Mango Cream, place mango flesh and coconut milk in a food processor or blender and process until smooth.

3 Preheat barbecue to a medium heat. Drain prawns (shrimp) and cook on lightly oiled barbecue for 3-4 minutes or until prawns change colour. Serve immediately with Mango Cream.

Coconut milk: This can be purchased in a number of forms: canned, as a long-life product in cartons, or as a powder to which you add water. Once opened it has a short life and should be used within a day or so. It is available from Asian food stores and some supermarkets, however if you have trouble finding it you can easily make your own. To make coconut milk, place 500 g/1 lb desiccated coconut in a bowl and add 3 cups/750mL/1 1/4pt of boiling water. Set aside to stand for 30 minutes, then strain, squeezing the coconut to extract as much liquid as possible. This will make a thick coconut milk. The coconut can be used again to make a weaker coconut milk.

Serves 6

ingredients

1 1/2kg/3 lb uncooked large prawns, (shrimp) peeled and deveined with tails left intact

Chilli marinade
2 teaspoons cracked black pepper
2 tablespoons sweet chilli sauce
1 tablespoon soy sauce
1 clove garlic, crushed
1/4 cup/60 mL/2 fl oz lemon juice

Mango cream
1 mango, peeled, stoned and roughly chopped
3 tablespoons coconut milk

salmon
cutlets with pineapple salsa

Method:

1 Preheat barbecue to a medium heat. Cook salmon cutlets on lightly oiled barbecue for 3-5 minutes each side or until flesh flakes when tested with a fork.

2 To make salsa, place pineapple, spring onions, chilli, lemon juice and mint in a food processor or blender and process to combine. Serve at room temperature with salmon cutlets.

Cook's tip: If fresh pineapple is unavailable use a can of drained crushed pineapple in natural juice in its place.

Note: This salsa is delicious served with any fish or barbecued chicken.

Serves 4

ingredients

4 salmon cutlets, cut 2½cm/1 in thick

Pineapple salsa
250g/8oz roughly chopped fresh pineapple
2 spring onions, finely chopped
1 fresh red chilli, seeded and finely chopped
1 tablespoon lemon juice
2 tablespoons finely chopped fresh mint

squid
and scallop salad

Method:

1. To make dressing, place ginger, rosemary, garlic, oil, lime juice and vinegar in a screwtop jar and shake well to combine. Set aside.

2. Preheat barbecue to a high heat. Place red and yellow or green pepper halves, skin side down on lightly oiled barbecue grill and cook for 5-10 minutes or until skins are blistered and charred. Place peppers in a plastic food bag or paper bag and set aside until cool enough to handle. Remove skins from peppers and cut flesh into thin strips.

3. Cut squid (calamari) tubes lengthwise and open out flat. Using a sharp knife cut parallel lines down the length of the squid (calamari), taking care not to cut through the flesh. Make more cuts in the opposite direction to form a diamond pattern. Cut into 5cm/2in squares.

4. Place squid (calamari) and scallops on lightly oiled barbecue plate (griddle) and cook, turning several times, for 3 minutes or until tender. Set aside to cool slightly.

5. Combine red and yellow or green peppers, asparagus, onion and coriander. Line a large serving platter with rocket or watercress, top with vegetables, squid (calamari) and scallops. Drizzle with dressing and serve immediately.

Serves 4

ingredients

1 red pepper, seeded and halved
1 yellow or green pepper, seeded and halved
2 squid (calamari) tubes
250g/8oz scallops, roe (coral) removed
250g/8oz asparagus, cut into 5cm/2in pieces, blanched
1 red onion, sliced
3 tablespoons fresh coriander leaves
1 bunch rocket or watercress

Herb and balsamic dressing
1 tablespoon finely grated fresh ginger
1 tablespoon chopped fresh rosemary
1 clove garlic, crushed
¼ cup/60mL/2fl oz olive oil
2 tablespoons lime juice
1 tablespoon balsamic or red wine vinegar

home
smoked trout

Method:

1 Place smoking chips and wine in a non-reactive metal dish and stand for 1 hour.
2 Preheat covered barbecue to a low heat. Place dish, with smoking chips in, in barbecue over hot coals, cover barbecue with lid and heat for 5-10 minutes or until liquid is hot.
3 Place trout on a wire rack set in a roasting tin. Brush trout lightly with oil, then top with onions, lemon and dill. Position roasting tin containing trout on rack in barbecue, cover barbecue with lid and smoke for 15-20 minutes or until trout flakes when tested with fork.

Note: This recipe is also suitable for a smoke box.

Serves 4

ingredients

1 cup/125g/4oz smoking chips
1/2 cup/125mL/4fl oz white wine
4 small rainbow trout, cleaned, with head and tail intact
1 tablespoon vegetable oil
3 red onions, thinly sliced
1 lemon, thinly sliced
8 sprigs dill

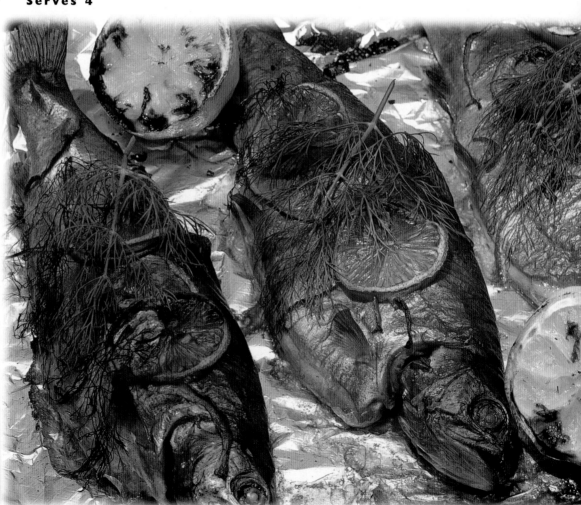

salmon
skewers

Method:

1 Preheat barbecue to a medium heat. Thread salmon and snow peas (mangetout), alternately, onto lightly oiled skewers.

2 Place mustard, thyme, cumin, lemon juice and honey in a bowl and mix to combine. Brush mustard mixture over salmon and cook on lightly oiled barbecue grill for 2-3 minutes each side or until salmon is just cooked.

Note: Watch a lit barbecue at all times and keep children and pets away from hot barbecues and equipment.

Serves 4

ingredients.

500g/1 lb salmon fillet, cut into 2¹/₂cm/1 in squares
250g/8oz snow peas (mangetout), trimmed
1 tablespoon wholegrain mustard
2 teaspoons chopped fresh lemon thyme or thyme
¹/₂ teaspoon ground cumin
2 tablespoons lemon juice
2 teaspoons honey

sesame prawn (shrimp) cakes

Photograph page 25

Method:

1 Preheat barbecue to a medium heat. Place prawns (shrimp), crab meat, spring onions, basil, chilli, cumin, paprika and egg white into a food processor and process until well combined. Take 4 tablespoons of mixture, shape into a pattie and roll in sesame seeds to coat. Repeat with remaining mixture to make six patties.

2 Heat oil on barbecue plate (griddle) for 2-3 minutes or until hot, add patties and cook for 10 minutes each side or until patties are golden and cooked.

Note: If fresh crab meat is unavailable drained canned crab can be used instead. These fish cakes are delicious served with a sweet chilli sauce for dipping. Sweet chilli sauce is available from Oriental food shops and some supermarkets.

Serves 6

ingredients

315g/10oz uncooked, shelled and deveined prawns (shrimp)
250g/8oz fresh crab meat
3 spring onions, chopped
2 tablespoons finely chopped fresh basil
1 fresh red chilli, finely chopped
1 teaspoon ground cumin
1 teaspoon paprika
1 egg white
155g/5oz sesame seeds
1 tablespoon vegetable oil

lemon grass prawns (shrimp)

salt

Photograph page 25

Method:

1 Wash prawns (shrimp), leaving shells and heads intact and place in a shallow glass or ceramic dish.

2 Place lemon grass, spring onions, chillies, garlic, ginger and shrimp paste in a food processor or blender and process until smooth. Add sugar and coconut milk and process to combine. Spoon mixture over prawns, toss to combine, cover and marinate in the refrigerator for 3-4 hours.

3 Preheat barbecue to a high heat. Drain prawns (shrimp), place on barbecue and cook, turning several times, for 5 minutes or until prawns (shrimp) change colour. Serve immediately.

Note: Fresh lemon grass and shrimp paste are available from Oriental food shops and some supermarkets. Lemon grass can also be purchased dried; if using dried lemon grass, soak it in hot water for 20 minutes or until soft before using.

Serves 4

ingredients

1 kg/2 lb uncooked medium prawns (shrimp)
3 stalks fresh lemon grass, finely chopped
2 spring onions, chopped
2 small fresh red chillies, finely chopped
2 cloves garlic, crushed
2 tablespoons finely grated fresh ginger
1 teaspoon shrimp paste
1 tablespoon brown sugar
1/2 cup/125mL/4fl oz coconut milk

blackened
tuna steaks

Method:

1 *Preheat barbecue to a high heat. To make salsa, place tomatoes, fennel, onion, capers, mint, garlic, lemon juice and orange juice in a bowl and toss to combine. Set aside until ready to serve.*

2 *To make spice mix, place paprika, ground garlic, onion powder, black peppercorns, herbs and cayenne pepper in a bowl and mix to combine. Add tuna, toss to coat and shake off excess.*

3 *Heat oil on barbecue plate (griddle) for 2-3 minutes or until hot, add tuna and cook for 3-4 minutes each side or until blackened and cooked to your liking. Serve immediately with salsa.*

Note: *If tuna is unavailable swordfish or salmon are delicious alternatives. Dried ground garlic is available in the spice section of supermarkets. It has a pungent taste and smell and should be used with care.*

Serves 4

ingredients

4 thick tuna steaks
2 tablespoons olive oil

Cajun spice mix
2 tablespoons sweet paprika
I tablespoon dried ground garlic
I tablespoon onion powder
2 teaspoons crushed black peppercorns
2 teaspoons dried mixed herbs
I teaspoon cayenne pepper

Fennel tomato salsa
4 plum (egg or Italian tomatoes), chopped
I bulb fennel, finely chopped
I red onion, finely chopped
2 tablespoons capers
I tablespoon chopped fresh mint
I clove garlic, crushed
I tablespoon lemon juice
I tablespoon orange juice

oysters
and mussels in shells

Method:

1 Preheat barbecue to a high heat. Place mussels and oysters on barbecue grill and cook for 3-5 minutes or until mussel shells open and oysters are warm. Discard any mussels that do not open after 5 minutes cooking.

2 Place butter, parsley, lemon juice, orange juice and wine in a heavy-based saucepan, place on barbecue and cook, stirring, for 2 minutes or until mixture is bubbling. Place mussels and oysters on a serving platter, drizzle with butter mixture and serve immediately.

Note: Mussels will live out of water for up to 7 days if treated correctly. To keep mussels alive, place them in a bucket, cover with a wet towel and top with ice. Store in a cool place and as the ice melts, drain off the water and replace ice. It is important that the mussels do not sit in the water or they will drown.

Serves 6

ingredients

**500g/1 lb mussels, scrubbed and beards removed
24 oysters in half shells
60g/2oz butter, softened
1 tablespoon chopped fresh parsley
2 tablespoons lemon juice
1 tablespoon orange juice
1 tablespoon white wine**

cranberry chicken skewers

perfect poultry

This exciting selection of recipes

for chicken, duck and quail are sure to become barbecue favourites. Included are such tempting dishes as Cranberry Chicken Skewers, Plum Duck Salad and Festive Smoked Turkey.

cranberry
chicken skewers

Photograph page 29

Method:

1 *Place ground chicken meat, breadcrumbs, onion, garlic, sage, mixed spice, egg and Tabasco sauce in a bowl and mix to combine.*

2 *Shape chicken mixture around lightly oiled skewers to form 7¹/₂cm/3in sausage shapes. Place skewers on a plate, cover and refrigerate for 2 hours.*

3 *Preheat barbecue to a medium heat. Place skewers on lightly oiled barbecue grill and cook, turning several times, for 5-10 minutes or until skewers are cooked. Drizzle with cranberry sauce and serve immediately.*

Note: *Remember always check the barbecue area before lighting the barbecue. Do not have the barbecue too close to the house and sweep up any dry leaves or anything that might catch fire if hit by a spark.*

Serves 6

ingredients

750g/1¹/₂ lb ground chicken meat
¹/₂ cup/30g/1oz breadcrumbs, made from stale bread
1 onion, diced
2 cloves garlic, crushed
2 tablespoons chopped fresh sage or
1 teaspoon dried sage
1 teaspoon ground mixed spice
1 egg, lightly beaten
¹/₄ teaspoon Tabasco sauce or according to taste
¹/₂ cup/125mL/4fl oz cranberry sauce, warmed

oriental
chicken livers

Method:

1 *To make marinade, place sugar and water in a bowl and mix to dissolve sugar. Add soy sauce, oyster sauce, five spice powder and garlic and mix to combine. Add chicken livers, cover and marinate in the refrigerator for 3 hours.*

2 *Preheat barbecue to a high heat. Drain livers well. Place a piece of liver and water chestnut on each piece of bacon and wrap to enclose. Secure with a wooden toothpick or cocktail stick. Place on lightly oiled barbecue grill and cook, turning several times, for 6-8 minutes or until bacon is crisp and livers are just cooked.*

Note: *Heat the barbecue plate (griddle) or grill and brush lightly with oil before adding the food. This will prevent the food sticking to the barbecue. Remember when brushing with oil to use a brush that can withstand heat - if you use one with nylon bristles they will melt.*

Makes 16

ingredients

125g/4oz chicken livers, trimmed, cleaned and cut into sixteen pieces
8 water chestnuts, halved
8 rashers bacon, rind removed and cut in half

Oriental marinade
1 teaspoon brown sugar
1 tablespoon hot water
2 tablespoons soy sauce
1 tablespoon oyster sauce
¹/₂ teaspoon five spice powder
2 cloves garlic, crushed

chilli
honey drumsticks

Method:

1 To make marinade, place lemon juice, honey, garlic and chilli powder in a bowl and mix to combine.

2 Place drumsticks in a shallow glass or ceramic dish, pour marinade over and toss to coat. Cover and marinate in the refrigerator for at least 2 hours, or overnight, turning several times during marinating.

3 Preheat barbecue to a medium heat. Drain drumsticks and reserve marinade. Cook drumsticks on lightly oiled barbecue, brushing frequently with marinade for 10-15 minutes, or until chicken is tender.

Serves 10

ingredients

10 chicken drumsticks

Chilli honey marinade
¹/₂ cup/125 mL/4fl oz lemon juice
¹/₂ cup/170g/5¹/₂oz honey
I clove garlic, crushed
pinch chilli powder

caribbean
spatchcock

Method:

1 To make marinade, place rum, lime rind, lime juice, honey, garlic and ginger in a bowl and mix to combine. Place spatchcock (poussin) halves in a shallow glass or ceramic dish and rub marinade into spatchcocks (poussins). Cover and set aside to marinate for 1 hour.

2 Preheat barbecue to a medium heat. Thread a skewer through wings and legs of each spatchcock (poussin) half and brush with any remaining marinade. Combine black pepper and coriander and press onto skin of birds. Cook on lightly oiled barbecue grill, turning frequently for 15-20 minutes or until birds are cooked through.

Cook's tip: This is also a delicious way to prepare and cook chicken pieces. Instead of using spatchcocks, simply use chicken pieces and prepare and marinate as in this recipe - the cooking time for the chicken pieces will be about the same as for the spatchcocks. You should cook them until the juices run clear.

Serves 6

ingredients

3 spatchcocks (poussins), halved
2 tablespoons cracked black pepper
1 teaspoon ground coriander

Lime marinade
3 tablespoons white rum
2 teaspoons finely grated lime rind
1 tablespoon lime juice
2 tablespoons honey
2 cloves garlic, crushed
1 teaspoon grated fresh ginger

cajun
chicken with lime sauce

Method:

1 Preheat barbecue to a high heat.
2 To make spice mix, place garlic, paprika, oregano, thyme, salt and black pepper in a bowl and mix to combine. Add chicken and toss to coat. Shake off excess spice mix and cook, turning frequently, on lightly oiled barbecue plate (griddle) for 5-7 minutes or until chicken is tender.
3 To make sauce, place yoghurt, lime juice, lime rind and cordial in a bowl and mix to combine. Serve with chicken.

Note: For an attractive presentation, place a bowl of dipping sauce in the centre of a serving platter, surround with chicken and garnish with lime wedges.

Serves 6

ingredients

4 boneless chicken breast fillets, cut into 2cm/³/₄in wide strips

Cajun spice mix
5 cloves garlic, crushed
4 tablespoons paprika
2 tablespoons dried oregano
2 tablespoons dried thyme
2 teaspoons salt
2 teaspoons freshly ground black pepper

Lime dipping
1¹/₂ cups/315g/10oz low-fat natural yoghurt
2 tablespoons fresh lime juice
1 tablespoon finely grated lime rind
1 teaspoon lime juice cordial

chilli
lime legs

Photograph page 35

ingredients

¹/₄ cup/60mL/2fl oz lime juice
¹/₄ cup/60mL/2fl oz buttermilk
2 tablespoons sweet chilli sauce
2 tablespoons reduced-salt soy sauce
12 chicken drumsticks, skinned

Method:

1 *Place lime juice, buttermilk, chilli sauce and soy sauce in a shallow glass or ceramic dish and mix to combine. Score each drumstick in several places, add to lime juice mixture, turn to coat, cover and marinate in the refrigerator for 3 hours.*

2 *Preheat barbecue to a medium heat. Drain chicken well and reserve marinade. Place chicken on lightly oiled barbecue grill and cook, basting frequently with reserved marinade and turning occasionally, for 25 minutes or until chicken is cooked.*

Note: *Buttermilk, which has a similar nutritional value to skim milk, is mildly acidic with a creamy taste and a thick consistency. A mixture of 2 tablespoons low-fat natural yogurt and 1 tablespoon reduced-fat milk can be used instead.*

Serves 6

buffalo
chilli chicken

Photograph page 35

ingredients

1 kg/2 lb chicken pieces, skinned
3 spring onions, chopped
2 cloves garlic, crushed
1 cup/250 mL/8 fl oz tomato sauce
¹/₄ cup/60mL/2fl oz beer
1 tablespoon cider vinegar
1 tablespoon honey
1 tablespoon Tabasco sauce or according to taste

Method:

1 *Score larger pieces of chicken at 2cm/³/₄in intervals and set aside.*

2 *Place spring onions, garlic, tomato sauce, beer, vinegar, honey and Tabasco sauce in a shallow glass or ceramic dish and mix to combine. Add chicken, toss to coat, cover and marinate in the refrigerator for 3-4 hours.*

3 *Preheat barbecue to a medium heat. Drain chicken and reserve marinade. Place chicken on lightly oiled barbecue grill and cook, basting frequently with reserved marinade and turning several times, for 10-15 minutes or until chicken is tender and cooked through.*

Note: *The cooking times for the chicken will vary according to the size of the pieces. If you have a variety of sizes, place the larger, longer cooking pieces such as drumsticks and thighs on the barbecue first and cook for 5 minutes, before adding the smaller quicker cooking pieces such as wings and breasts.*

Serves 4

chicken
with creamy pesto stuffing

Method:

1 *To make stuffing, place basil leaves, pine nuts and Parmesan cheese in a food processor and process to finely chopped. Stir basil mixture into cream cheese.*

2 *Cut through backbone of each chicken. Remove both halves of backbone, then turn chicken over and press to flatten.*

3 *Using your fingers or the handle of a wooden spoon, loosen skin over breasts, thighs and legs of chicken. Push stuffing under loosened skin, then thread skewers through wings and legs of chickens.*

4 *Preheat barbecue to a medium heat. Cook chicken on lightly oiled barbecue for 15-20 minutes each side or until chicken is cooked through.*

When is the chicken cooked?

To test your chicken for doneness pierce the thickest part of the chicken at the thigh joint and when the juices run clear the bird is cooked.

Serves 10

ingredients

3 x 1 ½ kg/3 lb chickens

Creaming pesto stuffing
90g/3oz basil leaves
60g/2oz pine nuts
½ cup/60g/2oz finely grated Parmesan cheese
250g/8oz cream cheese, softened

undercover
chicken

Method:

1 Preheat covered barbecue to a medium heat. Wash chicken inside and out and pat dry with absorbent kitchen paper.

2 Place butter, garlic, chives and parsley in a bowl and mix to combine. Using your fingers, loosen skin on breast of chicken. Push butter mixture under skin and smooth out evenly. Place chicken on a wire rack set in a roasting tin and brush with oil. Place prosciutto or ham over chicken breast in a criss-cross pattern and secure in place with wooden toothpicks or cocktail sticks. Pour wine over chicken.

3 Place roasting tin on rack in barbecue, cover barbecue with lid and cook for 1 1/2 hours or until chicken is tender. Cover and stand for 10 minutes before carving.

Note: Do not handle cooked and uncooked meat and poultry at the same time. This encourages the transfer of bacteria from raw food to cooked food. Always make sure that you have a clean tray or dish to place barbecued food on - do not place it on the same dish as was used for holding it raw - unless it has been thoroughly washed in hot soapy water.

Serves 6

ingredients

1 1/2 kg/3 lb chicken, cleaned
125 g/4 oz butter, softened
1 clove garlic, crushed
2 tablespoons snipped fresh chives
2 tablespoons chopped fresh parsley
1 tablespoon olive oil
8 slices prosciutto or lean ham
1 cup/250mL/8fl oz white wine

tikka
skewers

Method:

1 Pierce fish strips several times with a fork and place in a shallow glass or ceramic dish.
2 To make marinade, place onion, garlic, ginger, cumin, garam masala, cardamom, turmeric, chilli powder, coriander and tomato paste (purée) in a food processor or blender and process until smooth. Add yoghurt and mix to combine. Spoon marinade over fish, toss to combine, cover and marinate in the refrigerator for 3 hours.
3 Preheat barbecue to a medium heat. Drain fish and thread onto lightly oiled skewers. Place skewers on lightly oiled barbecue grill and cook, turning several times, for 5-6 minutes or until fish is cooked.
4 To make raitha, place cucumber, mint and yoghurt in a bowl and mix to combine. Serve skewers with lemon wedges and raitha.
Note: When buying fish fillets look for those that are shiny and firm with a pleasant sea smell. Avoid those that are dull, soft, discoloured or oozing water when touched.

Serves 6

ingredients

750g/1¹/₂ lb firm white fish fillets, cut into 2cm/³/₄in wide strips
1 lemon, cut into wedges

Spicy yoghurt marinade
1 onion, chopped
4 cloves garlic, crushed
2 teaspoons finely grated fresh ginger
1 tablespoon ground cumin
1 tablespoon garam masala
3 cardamom pods, crushed
1 teaspoon ground turmeric
2 teaspoons chilli powder
2 teaspoons ground coriander
1 tablespoon tomato paste (purée)
1³/₄ cups/350g/11oz natural yogurt

Cucumber raitha
1 cucumber, finely chopped
1 tablespoon chopped fresh mint
1 cup/200g/6¹/₂oz natural yogurt

fragrant
orange quail

Method:

1 To make marinade, place herbs, mustard, orange rind, garlic, cider, orange juice, brandy and oil in a shallow glass or ceramic dish and mix to combine. Add quail, turn to coat, cover and marinate in the refrigerator for 2 hours.

2 Preheat barbecue to a medium heat. Drain quail, place skin side up, on lightly oiled barbecue grill and cook, turning occasionally, for 10 minutes or until quail is tender.

3 For couscous, place couscous in a bowl, pour over boiling water, cover and set aside to stand for 10 minutes or until water is absorbed. Toss with a fork, add sultanas, hazelnuts, spring onions and lemon juice and toss to combine. To serve, line a large serving platter with couscous then arrange quail attractively on top.

Note: Often thought of as a type of grain couscous is actually a pasta made from durum wheat, however cook and use it in the same way as a grain. The name couscous refers to both the raw product and the cooked dish. It is an excellent source of thiamin and iron as well as being a good source of protein and niacin.

Serves 4

ingredients

6 quail, halved

<u>**Brandy orange marinade**</u>
6 tablespoons chopped fresh mixed herbs
2 tablespoons Dijon mustard
1 tablespoon finely grated orange rind
2 cloves garlic, crushed
¹/₂ cup/125mL/4fl oz cider
¹/₂ cup/125mL/4fl oz orange juice
¹/₄ cup/60mL/2fl oz brandy
1 tablespoon macadamia or walnut oil

<u>**Nutty couscous**</u>
1 cup/185g/6oz couscous
2 cups/500mL/16fl oz boiling water
90g/3oz sultanas
60g/2oz hazelnuts, toasted and chopped
2 spring onions, chopped
1 tablespoon lemon juice

chicken
in coals

Photograph page 41

ingredients

1 ¹/₂ kg/3 lb chicken
60g/2oz butter, melted
2 tablespoons soy sauce
1 tablespoon honey
2 star anise
1 cinnamon stick

Method:

1 Heat barbecue until flames die down and coals are glowing. The barbecue is ready when you can hold your hand about 10cm/ 4in from the coals for 4-5 seconds.

2 Cut chicken down back bone and press to flatten. Place butter, soy sauce and honey in a bowl and mix to combine. Brush butter mixture over chicken and place on a sheet of nonstick baking paper large enough to completely enclose chicken. Top chicken with star anise and cinnamon stick and wrap in baking paper. Then wrap paper parcel in a double thickness of aluminium foil.

3 Place chicken in coals and cook, turning several times, for 45-60 minutes or until chicken is cooked and tender.

Note: For this recipe the chicken is actually cooked in the coals of the barbecue so it is important that the fire is not too hot. If using wood the fire should burn down to red hot glowing embers. When using charcoal or heat beads the coals should be glowing and partially covered by grey ash. Charcoal takes 15-20 minutes to reach this stage, heat beads 30-40 minutes and wood an hour or more, depending on the variety used.

Serves 4

indian
yoghurt kebabs

Photograph page 41

ingredients

6 chicken thigh fillets, halved

Yoghurt marinade
1 tablespoon chopped fresh coriander
2 teaspoons finely grated fresh ginger
1 clove garlic, crushed
2 teaspoons paprika
1 teaspoon ground cumin
¹/₂ teaspoon ground turmeric
¹/₂ teaspoon chilli powder
¹/₂ teaspoon ground cinnamon
1 cup/200g/6¹/₂oz natural yoghurt
2 tablespoons lemon juice

Method:

1 To make marinade, place coriander, ginger, garlic, paprika, cumin, turmeric, chilli powder, cinnamon, yoghurt and lemon juice in a shallow glass or ceramic dish and mix well to combine. Add chicken, toss to coat and marinate at room temperature for 30 minutes.

2 Preheat barbecue to a medium heat. Drain chicken and thread three pieces onto a lightly oiled skewer. Repeat with remaining chicken to make four kebabs. Place kebabs on lightly oiled barbecue grill and cook for 4-5 minutes each side or until chicken is cooked and tender.

Note: If chicken thigh fillets are unavailable chicken breast fillets can be used instead. You will need 3 boneless chicken breast fillets, each cut into four pieces.

Serves 4

festive
smoked turkey

Method:

1 Soak smoking chips in brandy in a non-reactive metal dish for 1 hour.

2 To make stuffing, melt butter in a frying pan over a medium heat, add leek and spring onions and cook, stirring, for 3 minutes. Add bacon and cook for 5 minutes longer. Add breadcrumbs, pecans and sage and cook, stirring, for 5 minutes or until breadcrumbs are crisp. Remove from heat, add rice and mix to combine.

3 Preheat covered barbecue to a medium heat. Place dish, with smoking chips in, in barbecue over hot coals, cover barbecue with lid and heat for 5-10 minutes or until liquid is hot.

4 Spoon stuffing into body cavity of turkey. Secure openings with metal or bamboo skewers. Tuck wings under body and tie legs together. Place turkey on a wire rack set in a roasting tin. Combine stock and oil and brush over turkey.

5 Position roasting tin containing turkey on rack in barbecue, cover barbecue with lid and smoke, basting frequently, for 2½-3 hours or until turkey is cooked.

Note: Disposable aluminium foil trays available from supermarkets are ideal for putting the smoking chips in. The quantity of smoking chips used will determine the final flavour of the smoked food. For a guide follow the manufacturer's instructions, but don't be afraid to experiment.

Serves 8

ingredients

1 cup/125g/4oz smoking chips
½ cup/125mL/4fl oz brandy
3 kg/6 lb turkey, neck and giblets removed, trimmed of excess fat
½ cup/125mL/4fl oz chicken stock
2 tablespoons vegetable oil

Sage and rice stuffing
60g/2oz butter
1 leek, thinly sliced
4 spring onions chopped
3 rashers bacon, chopped
1 cup/60g/2oz breadcrumbs, made from stale bread
60g/2oz pecans, chopped
2 tablespoons chopped fresh sage or
1 teaspoon dried sage
1½ cups/280g/9oz rice, cooked

plum
duck salad

Method:

1 To make marinade, place ginger, mustard, garlic, plum sauce, vinegar and oil in a shallow glass or ceramic dish and mix to combine. Add duck and onions, turn to coat, cover and marinate in the refrigerator for 4 hours.

2 Preheat barbecue to a medium heat. Drain duck and onions well and reserve marinade. Place duck and onions on lightly oiled barbecue plate (griddle) and cook, basting frequently with reserved marinade and turning occasionally, for 10 minutes or until duck is tender. Set aside to cool slightly, then cut duck into thin slices.

3 Line a serving platter with lettuce and snow peas (mangetout), top with duck, onions, Camembert cheese, raspberries and almonds and toss gently to combine.

4 To make dressing, place orange juice, oil, vinegar and mustard in a bowl and whisk to combine. Drizzle dressing over salad and serve immediately.

Note: Mizuna lettuce has a long thin jagged leaf and makes a pretty base for this salad. If it is unavailable any soft leaf lettuce of your choice is a suitable alternative.

Serves 6

ingredients

3 duck breasts, skinned
2 onions, thinly sliced
1 mizuna lettuce, leaves separated
**185g/6oz snow peas (mangetout),
cut into thin strips**
185g/6oz Camembert cheese, sliced
185g/6oz raspberries
60g/2oz raw almonds, roasted

Mustard marinade
1 tablespoon grated fresh ginger
1 tablespoon wholegrain mustard
1 clove garlic, crushed
1/4 cup/60mL/2fl oz plum sauce
**1 tablespoon raspberry or
white wine vinegar**
1 tablespoon vegetable oil

Orange dressing
1/4 cup/60mL/2fl oz orange juice
2 tablespoons vegetable oil
1 tablespoon raspberry vinegar
1 tablespoon Dijon mustard

43

thai lamb noodle salad

make
· mine
meat

Here you will find new ways to

make the most of your favourite cuts of
meat. Why not try a Marinated Leg of Lamb
or Mixed Satays at your next barbecue.

thai lamb
and noodle salad

Photograph page 45

Method:

1 Combine lemon grass, garlic, lime juice, oil, chilli sauce and fish sauce in a glass or ceramic dish and mix to combine. Add lamb, turn to coat, cover and marinate in the refrigerator for 3 hours.
2 Preheat barbecue to a medium heat. To make salad, prepare noodles according to packet directions. Drain and place in a bowl. Add spring onions, red pepper, bean sprouts and coriander and toss to combine. Set aside.
3 To make dressing, place lime juice, fish sauce, honey and chilli powder in a screwtop jar and shake well to combine. Set aside.
4 Drain lamb and cook on lightly oiled barbecue, turning several times, for 5-10 minutes or until cooked to your liking. Slice lamb diagonally into 2cm/³⁄₄in thick slices.
5 To serve, place salad on a large serving platter, arrange lamb attractively on top and drizzle with dressing. Serve immediately.
Note: Rice noodles, also called rice vermicelli or rice sticks, vary in size from a narrow vermicelli style to a ribbon noodle about 5 mm/1/4 in wide. Made from rice flour, the noodles should be soaked before using; the narrow noodles require about 10 minutes soaking, while the wider ones will need about 30 minutes.

Serves 6

ingredients

1 stalk fresh lemon grass, chopped or ¹⁄₂ teaspoon dried lemon grass, soaked in hot water until soft
2 cloves garlic, crushed
¹⁄₄ cup/60mL/2fl oz lime juice
2 tablespoons vegetable oil
2 tablespoons sweet chilli sauce
1 tablespoon fish sauce
750g/1¹⁄₂ lb lamb fillets, trimmed of excess fat and sinew

Rice noodle salad
155g/5oz rice noodles
6 spring onions, chopped
1 red pepper, chopped
60g/2oz bean sprouts
3 tablespoons fresh coriander leaves

Lime and chilli dressing
¹⁄₄ cup/60mL/2fl oz lime juice
1 tablespoon fish sauce
1 tablespoon honey
pinch chilli powder or according to taste

lamb
with honeyed onions

Method:

1 To make marinade, place mint, garlic, yoghurt, mustard and mint sauce in a shallow glass or ceramic dish and mix to combine. Add lamb, turn to coat, cover and marinate in the refrigerator for 3 hours.

2 Preheat barbecue to a medium heat. For Honeyed Onions, heat oil on barbecue plate (griddle), add onions and cook, stirring constantly, for 10 minutes. Add honey and vinegar and cook, stirring, for 5 minutes longer or until onions are very soft and golden.

3 Drain lamb, place on lightly oiled barbecue and cook for 2-3 minutes each side or until cooked to your liking. Serve with onions.

Note: Before lighting a gas barbecue check that all the gas fittings and hose connections are tight and fitting correctly.

Serves 6

ingredients

12 lamb cutlets, trimmed of excess fat

Yoghurt marinade
1 tablespoon chopped fresh mint
1 clove garlic, crushed
1 cup/200 g/61/2 oz low-fat natural yoghurt
2 tablespoons wholegrain mustard
1 tablespoon prepared mint sauce

Honeyed onions
2 tablespoons olive oil
2 red onions, sliced
1 tablespoon honey
2 tablespoons red wine vinegar

mixed
satays

Method:

1 Weave chicken, beef and pork strips onto skewers and place in a shallow glass or ceramic dish.

2 To make marinade, place soy sauce, lime or lemon juice, garlic, ginger, chilli and coriander in a small bowl and mix to combine. Pour marinade over skewers in dish, cover and set aside to marinate for at least 1 hour.

3 Preheat barbecue to a medium heat. Cook kebabs on lightly oiled barbecue, turning frequently for 5-6 minutes, or until meats are cooked.

4 To make sauce, place peanut butter, onion, hoisin sauce, garlic and coconut milk in a food processor or blender and process until smooth. Stir in coriander. Serve with skewers for dipping.

Makes 12 skewers

ingredients

250g/8oz chicken breast fillets, skin removed and sliced into thin strips, lengthwise
250g/8oz beef fillet, sliced into thin strips, lengthwise
250g/8oz pork fillet, sliced into thin strips, lengthwise
12 skewers, lightly oiled

Chilli marinade
1/4 cup/60mL/2fl oz soy sauce
2 tablespoons lime or lemon juice
2 cloves garlic, crushed
2 teaspoons finely grated fresh ginger
1 fresh red chilli, finely chopped
1 tablespoon finely chopped fresh coriander

Peanut sauce
1/2 cup/125g/4oz crunchy peanut butter
1 onion, finely chopped
2 tablespoons hoisin sauce
2 cloves garlic, crushed
1/2 cup/125mL/4fl oz coconut milk
2 tablespoons finely chopped fresh coriander

barbecued
steak sandwiches

Method:

1 To make marinade, place wine, oil, garlic and ginger in a bowl and mix to combine. Place steaks in a shallow glass or ceramic dish. Pour marinade over, cover, and marinate at room temperature for 2-3 hours or overnight in the refrigerator.

2 Cook onions on lightly oiled barbecue plate (griddle) or in a lightly oiled frying pan on barbecue for 10-15 minutes or until golden. Preheat barbecue to a medium heat. Drain steaks and cook on lightly oiled barbecue for 3-5 minutes each side or until cooked to your liking.

3 Lightly brush bread slices with oil and cook on barbecue grill for 1-2 minutes each side or until lightly toasted. To assemble sandwiches, top 6 toasted bread slices with steak, onions and remaining bread slices.

Cook's tip: You may like to add some salad ingredients to your sandwiches. Mustard or relish is also a tasty addition.

Marinated steak, barbecued and placed between slices of grilled bread makes the best steak sandwiches you will ever taste.

Serves 6

ingredients

6 lean rump steaks, cut 1cm/¹/₂in thick
3 onions, finely sliced
12 thick slices wholemeal or grain bread
olive oil

<u>Ginger wine marinade</u>
1 cup/250mL/8fl oz red wine
¹/₂ cup/125mL/4fl oz olive oil
1 clove garlic, crushed
2 teaspoons grated fresh ginger

lamb
cutlets with honey butter

Method:

1 *To make Honey Butter, place butter, mint, honey and black pepper to taste in a small bowl and mix to combine. Place mixture on plastic food wrap and roll into a cylindrical shape. Refrigerate until hard.*

2 *Preheat barbecue to a medium heat. Place oil and garlic in a small bowl and mix to combine. Wrap ends of cutlet bones in aluminium foil to prevent burning during cooking. Brush cutlets with oil mixture and cook on barbecue plate (griddle) for 3 minutes each side or until lamb is tender.*

3 *Cut butter into small rounds and serve with cutlets.*

Cook's tip: *Interesting butter shapes can be made by using small cookie cutter shapes.*

Serves 4

ingredients

1 tablespoon vegetable oil
1 clove garlic, crushed
8 lamb cutlets

<u>Honey butter</u>
90g/3oz butter, softened
2 tablespoons chopped fresh mint
1 tablespoon honey
freshly ground black pepper

pork steaks
with apple stuffing

Method:

1 Place butterfly steaks on a board and, using a meat mallet, flatten slightly.
2 To make stuffing, melt butter in a frying pan and cook onion and bacon for 4-5 minutes or until bacon is crisp. Add apple and cook until apple is soft. Place apple mixture in a bowl, add bread crumbs, egg, mozzarella cheese and parsley and mix to combine. Season to taste with black pepper.
3 Preheat barbecue to a medium heat. Place spoonfuls of stuffing on one side of each butterfly steak, then fold over and secure with toothpicks. Cook on lightly oiled barbecue for 5-6 minutes each side or until steaks are cooked.

Serves 6

ingredients

6 pork butterfly steaks

Apple stuffing
30g/1oz butter
1 onion, finely chopped
2 rashers bacon, finely chopped
1 apple, cored and finely chopped
1 ½ cups/90g/3oz bread crumbs, made from stale bread
1 egg, lightly beaten
155g/5oz mozzarella cheese, cut into small cubes
2 tablespoons chopped fresh parsley
freshly ground black pepper

fruity
barbecued lamb

Photograph page 53

Method:

1 *Score the thickest part of each lamb shank (knuckle) to allow for even cooking.*
2 *Place chutney, crushed garlic, ginger, apple juice, wine and oil in a shallow ovenproof glass, ceramic or enamel dish and mix to combine. Add lamb, turn to coat, cover and marinate in the refrigerator for 2 hours. Remove lamb from refrigerator and bake in oven for 1 hour.*
3 *Preheat barbecue to a medium heat. Remove lamb from baking dish and place on lightly oiled barbecue, add garlic bulbs and cook, turning occasionally, for 30 minutes or until lamb and garlic are tender.*

Note: *Use fresh young garlic for this recipe, its flavour is milder than more mature garlic and when cooked develops a delicious nutty taste. Lamb chops are also delicious cooked in this way, however no precooking is required and the cooking time on the barbecue will only be 3-5 minutes each side.*

Serves 4

ingredients

4 lamb shanks (knuckles)
2 tablespoons mango chutney
2 cloves garlic, crushed
1 tablespoon finely grated fresh ginger
$^1/_4$ cup/60mL/2fl oz apple juice
$^1/_4$ cup/60ml/2fl oz white wine
2 tablespoons olive oil
**4 bulbs young garlic,
cut in half horizontally**

Oven temperature 180°C, 350°F, Gas 4

rosemary
and thyme chops

Photograph page 53

Method:

1 *To make marinade, place rosemary, thyme, garlic, oil, vinegar and lime juice in a shallow glass or ceramic dish and mix to combine. Add lamb, turn to coat, cover and marinate at room temperature for 1 hour.*
2 *Preheat barbecue to a high heat. Drain lamb, place on lightly oiled barbecue and cook for 3-5 minutes each side or until chops are cooked to your liking.*

Note: *Long-handled tongs are a must for turning food without burning your hands.*

Serves 6

ingredients

**12 lamb neck chops, trimmed
of excess fat**

Fresh herb marinade
2 tablespoons chopped fresh rosemary
2 tablespoons chopped fresh thyme
2 cloves garlic, crushed
$^1/_4$ cup/60mL/2fl oz olive oil
**$^1/_4$ cup/60mL/2fl oz balsamic or
red wine vinegar**
2 tablespoons lime juice

marinated
leg of lamb

Method:

1 *Lay lamb out flat and season well with black pepper. Place in a shallow glass or ceramic dish.*

2 *To make marinade, place garlic, oil, lemon juice, marjoram and thyme in a small bowl and mix to combine. Pour marinade over lamb, cover and allow to marinate at room temperature for 3-4 hours, or overnight in the refrigerator.*

3 *Preheat barbecue to a medium heat. Remove lamb from marinade and reserve marinade. Cook lamb on lightly oiled barbecue grill, turning several times during cooking and basting with reserved marinade, for 15-25 minutes or until cooked to your liking.*

Cook's tip: *Try lemon thyme instead of ordinary thyme in this recipe. Your butcher will butterfly the leg in minutes for you, or you can do it yourself.*

Serves 6

ingredients

1 ¹/₂-2 kg/3-4 lb leg of lamb, butterflied freshly ground black pepper

Lemon herb marinade
2 cloves garlic, crushed
¹/₄ cup/60mL/2fl oz olive oil
¹/₄ cup/60mL/2fl oz lemon juice
1 tablespoon finely chopped fresh marjoram or 1 teaspoon dried marjoram
1 tablespoon finely chopped fresh thyme or 1 teaspoon dried thyme

hot chilli
pork spareribs

Method:

1 Season ribs with black pepper and place in a shallow glass or ceramic dish. Combine apple juice, lime juice and Tabasco sauce, pour over ribs and toss to coat. Cover and refrigerate for 1-2 hours.

2 To make glaze, heat oil in a saucepan and cook onions, garlic and chilli over a medium heat for 10 minutes or until onions are soft. Stir in apple purée, jelly and juice, bring to simmering and simmer, stirring frequently, for 15 minutes or until mixture thickens. Stir in lime juice and season to taste with black pepper and cook for 15 minutes longer or until mixture thickens.

3 Preheat barbecue to a medium heat. Drain ribs and sear on lightly oiled barbecue for 5 minutes each side, brushing with reserved apple juice mixture frequently. Brush ribs with warm glaze and cook, turning, for 5 minutes longer. Serve ribs with remaining glaze.

Note: Apple, pork and chilli combine for the tastiest spareribs ever.

Serves 6

ingredients

6 small pork back rib racks
freshly ground black pepper
¹/₂ cup/125mL/4fl oz apple juice
¹/₄ cup/60mL/2fl oz lime juice
dash Tabasco sauce

Apple chilli glaze
1 tablespoons vegetable oil
2 onions, finely chopped
2 cloves garlic, crushed
1 fresh red chilli, seeded
and finely chopped
125g/4oz canned apple purée
1 cup/315g/10oz apple jelly
¹/₂ cup/125mL/4fl oz apple juice
2 tablespoons lime juice
freshly ground black pepper

steaks
with blue butter

Method:

1 *To make Blue Butter, place butter, blue cheese, parsley and paprika in a bowl and beat to combine. Place butter on a piece of plastic food wrap and roll into a log shape. Refrigerate for 1 hour or until firm.*

2 *Preheat barbecue to a high heat.*

3 *Place black pepper and oil in a bowl and mix to combine. Brush steaks lightly with oil mixture. Place steaks on lightly oiled barbecue grill and cook for 3-5 minutes each side or until steaks are cooked to your liking.*

4 *Cut butter into 2cm/³/₄in thick slices and top each steak with 1 or 2 slices. Serve immediately.*
Note: *Any leftover Blue Butter can be stored in the freezer to use at a later date. It is also delicious served with grilled lamb chops or cutlets and grilled vegetables such as eggplant (aubergine), red and green peppers and zucchini (courgettes).*
Serves 6

ingredients

**1 tablespoon freshly ground
black pepper
2 tablespoons olive oil
6 fillet steaks, trimmed of excess fat**

Blue butter
**125g/4oz butter, softened
60g/2oz blue cheese
1 tablespoon chopped fresh parsley
1 teaspoon paprika**

beef
and bacon burgers

Method:

1 Preheat barbecue to a medium heat. Place beef, spring onions, chives, egg, tomato sauce, Worcestershire sauce and chilli sauce in a bowl and mix to combine. Shape mixture into twelve patties. Top six patties with mozzarella cheese, then with remaining patties and pinch edges together to seal. Wrap a piece of bacon around each pattie and secure with a wooden toothpick or cocktail stick. Place on a plate and refrigerate for 2 hours or until patties are firm.

2 Place patties in a lightly oiled hinged wire barbecue frame and cook on barbecue grill for 10-15 minutes or until patties are cooked to your liking and cheese melts.

Note: A hinged wire frame is a useful barbecue accessory. It is ideal for cooking fragile and delicate foods such as fish - whole, fillets and cutlets - and burgers which can fall apart when turning.

Serves 6

ingredients

750g/1 1/2 lb lean ground beef
3 spring onions, chopped
2 tablespoons snipped fresh chives
1 egg, lightly beaten
2 tablespoons tomato sauce
1 tablespoon Worcestershire sauce
1 tablespoon chilli sauce
125g/4oz grated mozzarella cheese
6 rashers bacon, rind removed

cajun
spiced steaks

Method:

1 Preheat barbecue to a high heat. To make salsa, place pineapple, spring onions, coriander, chilli, sugar and vinegar in a bowl and toss to combine. Set aside.

2 To make spice mixture, combine paprika, black peppercorns, thyme, oregano and chilli powder. Rub spice mixture over steaks. Place steaks on lightly oiled barbecue and cook for 3-5 minutes each side or until cooked to your liking. Serve with salsa.

Note: When testing to see if a steak is cooked to your liking, press it with a pair of blunt tongs. Do not cut the meat, as this causes the juices to escape. Rare steaks will feel springy, medium steaks slightly springy and well-done steaks will feel firm. As a guide a 2.5 cm/1 in thick steak cooked to rare takes about 3 minutes each side, a medium steak 4 minutes and a well-done steak 5 minutes.

Serves 4

ingredients

4 sirloin or fillet steaks, trimmed of excess fat

Cajun spice mixture
1 tablespoon sweet paprika
1 teaspoon crushed black peppercorns
1 teaspoon ground thyme
1 teaspoon ground oregano
1/4 teaspoon chilli powder

Pineapple chilli salsa
1/2 pineapple, peeled and chopped
2 spring onions, chopped
1 tablespoon chopped fresh coriander
1 fresh red chilli, chopped
1 tablespoon brown sugar
1 tablespoon white vinegar

korean
bulgogi

Method:

1 Place garlic, ginger, soy sauce, honey and chilli sauce in a bowl and mix to combine. Add beef, toss to coat, cover and marinate in the refrigerator for 4 hours.

2 Preheat barbecue to a high heat. Heat 1 tablespoon oil on barbecue plate (griddle), add beef and stir-fry for 1-2 minutes or until beef just changes colour. Push beef to side of barbecue to keep warm.

3 Heat remaining oil on barbecue plate (griddle), add onions and bean sprouts and stir-fry for 4-5 minutes or until onions are golden. Add beef to onion mixture and stir-fry for 1-2 minutes longer. Sprinkle with sesame seeds and serve immediately.

Note: Serve with steamed white or brown rice and a tossed green salad.

Serves 6

ingredients

4 cloves garlic, crushed
2 teaspoons finely grated fresh ginger
¹/₄ cup/60mL/2fl oz soy sauce
3 tablespoons honey
1 tablespoon sweet chilli sauce
750g/1¹/₂ lb rump steak, trimmed of visible fat and thinly sliced
2 tablespoons vegetable oil
2 onions, sliced
125g/4oz bean sprouts
2 tablespoons sesame seeds

barbecued pumpkin pizza

vegetaria
variety

Given the number of people who now

choose to be vegetarians or semi-vegetarians it is a good idea to serve a vegetarian alternative - these recipes fit the bill and are sure to be popular with everyone.

basic
pizza dough

ingredients

1 teaspoon active dry yeast
pinch sugar
²/₃ cup/170mL/5¹/₂fl oz warm water
2 cups/250g/8oz flour
¹/₂ teaspoon salt
¹/₄ cup/60mL/2fl oz olive oil

Method:

1 *Place yeast, sugar and water in a bowl and mix to dissolve. Set aside in a warm, draught-free place for 5 minutes or until mixture is foamy.*

2 *Place flour and salt in a food processor and pulse once or twice to sift. With machine running, slowly pour in yeast mixture and oil and process to form a rough dough. Turn dough onto a lightly floured surface and knead for 5 minutes or until soft and shiny. Add more flour if necessary.*

3 *Place dough in a lightly oiled large bowl, roll dough around bowl to cover surface with oil. Cover bowl with plastic food wrap and place in a warm draught-free place for 1-1¹/₂ hours or until doubled in size. Knock down, knead lightly and use as desired.*

Note: *There are two types of yeast commonly used in bread-making - fresh and dry. Dry yeast is twice as concentrated as fresh yeast. You will find that 15g/¹/₂oz dry yeast has the same raising power as 30g/1oz fresh yeast.*

Makes enough dough for 4 individual pizzas or 1 large pizza

barbecued
pumpkin pizza

Photograph page 61

ingredients

1 quantity Basic Pizza Dough (as above)

Pumpkin feta topping
1 tablespoon olive oil
8 large slices pumpkin, peeled and seeds removed
1 onion, sliced
315g/10oz feta cheese, crumbled
1 tablespoon chopped fresh thyme
freshly ground black pepper

Method:

1 *Preheat barbecue to a high heat. To make topping, heat oil on barbecue plate (griddle) for 2-3 minutes or until hot, add pumpkin and onion and cook for 5 minutes each side or until soft and golden. Set aside.*

2 *Divide dough into four portions and roll into rounds 3mm/¹/₈in thick. Place dough rounds on lightly oiled barbecue and cook for 3-5 minutes or until brown and crisp. Turn over, top with pumpkin, onion, feta cheese, thyme and black pepper to taste and cook for 4-6 minutes longer or until pizza crust is crisp, golden and cooked through. Serve immediately.*

Note: *Orange sweet potatoes make a delicious alternative to the pumpkin in this recipe.*

Serves 4

char-grilled
mushrooms and toast

Method:

1 Preheat barbecue to a medium heat. Brush mushrooms with oil and cook on lightly oiled barbecue for 4-5 minutes or until cooked. Brush both sides of the bread with remaining oil and cook for 2-3 minutes each side or until golden.

2 Rub one side of each bread slice with cut side of garlic clove. Top each slice of bread with mushrooms, sprinkle with parsley, chives and basil. Season to taste with black pepper and serve immediately.

Note: This delicious first course takes only minutes to cook.

Serves 2

ingredients

6 flat mushrooms
¹/₄ cup/60mL/2fl oz olive oil
2 thick slices of bread
1 clove garlic, cut in half
2 teaspoons finely chopped fresh parsley
2 teaspoons snipped fresh chives
1 teaspoon finely chopped fresh basil
freshly ground black pepper

vegetable
burgers

Method:

1 To make patties, boil, steam or microwave broccoli, zucchini (courgettes) and carrots until tender. Drain, rinse under cold running water and pat dry.

2 Place broccoli, zucchini (courgettes), carrots, onions, garlic and parsley in a food processor and process until puréed. Transfer vegetable mixture to a mixing bowl, add bread crumbs and flour, season with black pepper and mix to combine. Cover and refrigerate for 30 minutes.

3 Shape mixture into ten patties. Place on a tray lined with nonstick baking paper, cover and refrigerate until required.

4 To make sauce, heat oil in a saucepan and cook onion, garlic, chilli and green pepper for 5 minutes or until onion and green pepper are soft. Add tomatoes, bring mixture to the boil, then reduce heat and simmer for 15-20 minutes or until sauce thickens. Season to taste with black pepper.

5 Preheat barbecue to a medium heat. Cook patties on lightly oiled barbecue plate (griddle) or in a lightly oiled frying pan on barbecue for 3-4 minutes each side. Toast rolls on barbecue. Place a lettuce leaf, a pattie, and a spoonful of sauce on the bottom half of each roll, top with remaining roll half and serve immediately.

Makes 10 burgers

ingredients

10 wholemeal rolls, split
10 lettuce leaves

Mixed vegetable patties
500g/1 lb broccoli, chopped
500g/1 lb zucchini (courgettes), chopped
250g/8oz carrots, chopped
2 onions, finely chopped
2 cloves garlic, crushed
3 tablespoons chopped parsley
3 cups/185g/6oz dried bread crumbs
1/2 cup/60g/2oz flour, sifted
freshly ground black pepper

Spicy tomato sauce
1 tablespoon olive oil
1 onion, finely chopped
1 clove garlic, crushed
1 fresh red chilli, seeded and finely chopped
1 green pepper, finely chopped
440g/14oz canned tomatoes,
undrained and mashed
freshly ground black pepper

char-grilled
vegetable slices

Method:

1 *Preheat barbecue to a medium heat. Place oil and garlic in a small bowl and whisk to combine. Brush eggplant (aubergine) slices, zucchini (courgette) slices, red pepper slices and tomato slices with oil mixture.*

2 *Cook eggplant (aubergine), zucchini (courgette) and red pepper slices on lightly oiled barbecue, turning frequently, for 4-5 minutes or until almost cooked. Add tomato slices to barbecue and cook all vegetables for 2-3 minutes longer.*

Serves 6

ingredients

¹/₂ cup/125mL/4fl oz olive oil
1 clove garlic, crushed
1 large eggplant (aubergine), cut lengthwise into thick slices
3 large zucchini (courgettes), cut lengthwise into thick slices
2 red peppers, cut into quarters, seeds removed
3 large firm tomatoes, cut into thick slices
freshly ground black pepper

mushroom
risotto cakes

Method:

1 Melt butter and oil together in saucepan over a medium heat, add garlic and bacon and cook, stirring, for 3 minutes or until bacon is crisp. Add leek and cook for 3 minutes or until leek is golden. Add rice and mushrooms to pan and cook, stirring, for 3 minutes longer.

2 Stir in ³/₄ cup/185mL/6fl oz hot stock and ¹/₄ cup/60mL/2fl oz wine and cook, stirring constantly, over a medium heat until liquid is absorbed. Continue adding stock and wine in this way, stirring constantly and allowing liquid to be absorbed before adding more.

3 Remove pan from heat, add Parmesan cheese and black pepper to taste and mix to combine. Set aside to cool, then refrigerate for at least 3 hours.

4 Preheat barbecue to a medium heat. Shape tablespoons of rice mixture into patties. Toss in flour to coat and shake off excess. Dip patties in eggs and roll in breadcrumbs to coat. Cook patties on lightly oiled barbecue plate (griddle) for 5 minutes each side or until golden and heated through.

Note: These bite-sized morsels are sure to be a hit with drinks before any barbecue. They can also be cooked in a frying pan over a medium heat on the cooker top.

For a vegetarian version of this recipe omit the bacon and use vegetable stock.

ingredients

30g/1oz butter
1 tablespoon olive oil
2 cloves garlic, crushed
3 rashers bacon, chopped
1 leek, thinly sliced
1¹/₄ cups/280g/9oz Arborio or risotto rice
125g/4oz button mushrooms, sliced
3 cups/750mL/1¹/₄pt hot chicken or vegetable stock
1 cup/250mL/8fl oz dry white wine
60g/2oz grated Parmesan cheese
freshly ground black pepper
¹/₄ cup/30g/1oz flour
2 eggs, lightly beaten
1¹/₂ cups/90g/3oz wholemeal breadcrumbs, made from stale bread

Serves 6

wild
rice and bean patties

Method:

1 Preheat barbecue to a medium heat. Place soya beans, fresh coriander, spring onions, ginger, cumin, ground coriander and turmeric into a food processor and process for 30 seconds or until mixture resembles coarse breadcrumbs. Transfer mixture to a bowl, add rice, flour and egg and mix to combine. Shape mixture into patties.

2 Heat oil on barbecue plate (griddle) for 2-3 minutes or until hot, add patties and cook for 5 minutes each side or until golden and heated through.

3 To make chilli yoghurt, place yogurt, chilli sauce and lime juice in a bowl and mix to combine. Serve with patties.

Serves 6

ingredients

440g/14oz canned soya beans, drained and rinsed
6 tablespoons chopped fresh coriander
3 spring onions, chopped
1 tablespoon finely grated fresh ginger
1 tablespoon ground cumin
1 tablespoon ground coriander
¹/₂ teaspoon ground turmeric
¹/₂ cup/100g/3¹/₂oz wild rice blend, cooked
¹/₂ cup/75g/2¹/₂oz wholemeal flour
1 egg, lightly beaten
2 tablespoons vegetable oil

Sweet chilli yoghurt
1 cup/200g/6¹/₂oz low-fat natural yoghurt
2 tablespoons sweet chilli sauce
1 tablespoon lime juice

nutty
crusted ricotta salad

Method:

1 Place ricotta cheese in a colander lined with muslin and drain for 1 hour.
2 Preheat barbecue to a medium heat. Place Parmesan cheese, pine nuts, paprika, oregano and 2 tablespoons oil in a bowl and mix to combine. Press nut mixture over surface of ricotta cheese to coat.
3 Heat remaining oil on barbecue plate (griddle) until hot, then cook ricotta cheese, turning occasionally, for 10 minutes or until golden. Stand for 10 minutes, then cut into slices.
4 Line a large serving platter with salad leaves, then arrange snow pea (mangetout) sprouts or watercress, teardrop or cherry tomatoes, avocado, sun-dried tomatoes and ricotta cheese slices attractively on top.
5 To make dressing, place garlic, cumin, coriander, chilli flakes, oil, vinegar and honey in a bowl and whisk to combine. Drizzle over salad and serve.

Note: If a gas barbecue does not light first time, turn if off, wait 20 seconds and try again. This will ensure that there is no gas build-up.

Serves 4

ingredients

315g/10oz ricotta cheese in one piece
90g/3oz grated Parmesan cheese
60g/2oz pine nuts, toasted and finely chopped
1 tablespoon sweet paprika
1 tablespoon dried oregano
4 tablespoons olive oil
315g/10oz assorted salad leaves
90g/3oz snow pea (mangetout) sprouts or watercress
185g/6oz yellow teardrop or cherry tomatoes
1 avocado, stoned, peeled and chopped
30g/1oz sun-dried tomatoes, sliced

Spiced honey dressing
2 cloves garlic, crushed
1 teaspoon ground cumin
1 teaspoon ground coriander
pinch red chilli flakes
1/4 cup/60mL/2fl oz olive oil
1 tablespoon cider vinegar
1 teaspoon honey

couscous
filled mushrooms

Method:

1 Preheat barbecue to a high heat. Place couscous in a bowl, pour over boiling water, cover and set aside to stand for 5 minutes or until water is absorbed. Add butter and toss gently with a fork.

2 Heat oil in a frying pan over a medium heat, add onion and garlic and cook, stirring, for 3 minutes or until onion is soft. Add garam masala and cayenne pepper and cook for 1 minute longer. Add onion mixture to couscous and toss to combine.

3 Fill mushrooms with couscous mixture, top with feta cheese and cook on lightly oiled barbecue grill for 5 minutes or until mushrooms are tender and cheese melts.
Note: If your barbecue only has a grill, use a large long-handled frying pan when a recipe calls for food to be cooked on the barbecue plate (griddle).

Serves 4

ingredients

²/₃ cup/125g/4oz couscous
²/₃ cup/170mL/5¹/₂fl oz boiling water
15g/¹/₂oz butter
2 teaspoons olive oil
1 onion, chopped
2 cloves garlic, crushed
1 teaspoon garam masala
pinch cayenne pepper
12 large mushrooms, stalks removed
200g/6¹/₂oz feta cheese, crumbled

warm
vegetable salad

Photograph page 71

ingredients

**6 zucchini (courgettes),
cut lengthwise into quarters
2 red onions, sliced
155g/5oz snow pea (mangetout) sprouts
or watercress
1 yellow or red pepper, chopped
1 avocado, stoned, peeled and chopped**

Orange dressing
**2 tablespoons snipped fresh chives
¹/₄ cup/60mL/2fl oz orange juice
1 tablespoon white wine vinegar
2 teaspoons French mustard**

Method:
1 *Preheat barbecue to a medium heat. Place zucchini (courgettes) and onions on lightly oiled barbecue and cook for 2-3 minutes each side or until golden and tender.*
2 *Arrange snow pea (mangetout) sprouts or watercress, yellow or red pepper and avocado attractively on a serving platter. Top with zucchini (courgettes) and onions.*
3 *To make dressing, place chives, orange juice, vinegar and mustard in a screwtop jar and shake well to combine. Drizzle over salad and serve immediately.*
Note: *This salad is delicious served with toasted olive bread.*
Serves 4

kebabs
with herb sauce

Photograph page 71

ingredients

**1 green pepper, seeded and cut into
2cm/³/₄in squares
2 zucchini (courgettes), cut into 2cm/³/₄in pieces
1 red onion, cut into 2cm/³/₄in cubes
1 eggplant (aubergine), cut into 2cm/³/₄in cubes
16 cherry tomatoes
2 tablespoons olive oil
2 tablespoons lemon juice
1 tablespoon chopped fresh oregano or
1 teaspoon dried oregano**

Herb sauce
**1 tablespoon chopped fresh dill
2 tablespoons snipped fresh chives
1 cup/250g/8oz sour cream
2 tablespoons lemon juice**

Method:
1 *Preheat barbecue to a medium heat. Thread a piece of green pepper, zucchini (courgette), onion, eggplant (aubergine) and a tomato onto a lightly oiled skewer. Repeat with remaining vegetables to use all ingredients.*
2 *Combine oil, lemon juice and oregano and brush over kebabs. Place kebabs on lightly oiled barbecue grill and cook, turning several times, for 5-10 minutes or until vegetables are tender.*
3 *To make sauce, place dill, chives, sour cream and lemon juice in a bowl and mix to combine. Serve with kebabs.*
Note: *Always keep water close at hand when barbecuing. If a hose or tap is not close by, then have a bucket of water next to the barbecue. A fire extinguisher or fire blanket is also a sensible safety precaution.*
Serves 4

grilled
pepper polenta

Method:

1 Place water in a saucepan and bring to the boil. Reduce heat to simmering, then gradually whisk in corn meal (polenta) and cook, stirring, for 20 minutes or until mixture is thick and leaves the sides of the pan.

2 Stir in butter, black peppercorns and grated Parmesan cheese. Spread mixture evenly into a greased 18x28cm/7x11in shallow cake tin and refrigerate until set. Cut polenta in triangles.

3 Brush polenta and vegetables with oil, then cook under a preheated hot grill or on a barbecue grill for 3-5 minutes each side or until polenta is golden and vegetables are brown and tender.

4 To serve, top polenta triangles with rocket, grilled vegetables, pesto and Parmesan cheese shavings.

Note: When grilling or barbecuing polenta as in this recipe it is important that the polenta is placed on the preheated surface and left alone until a crust forms. Once the crust forms completely the polenta can easily be turned. Do not be tempted to try turning it too soon or the delicious crust will be left on the grill.

ingredients

8 cups/2 litres/3½ pt water
2 cups/350g/11oz corn meal (polenta)
125g/4oz butter, chopped
1 tablespoon crushed black peppercorns
125g/4oz grated Parmesan cheese
2 tablespoons olive oil
2 zucchini (courgettes), cut into strips
1 red pepper, cut into thin strips
1 eggplant (aubergine), cut into strips
125g/4oz rocket leaves
½ cup/125g/4oz ready-made pesto
fresh Parmesan cheese shavings

Serves 8

vegetable
skewers with tahini

Method:

1 Thread zucchini (courgettes), red and yellow or green peppers, squash and feta cheese onto lightly oiled skewers. Brush skewers with oil and cook on a preheated hot barbecue or under a hot grill for 2 minutes each side or until brown and vegetables are tender crisp.

2 To make dip, place tahini, yoghurt, lime juice, chilli sauce, tomato paste (purée) and black pepper to taste in a bowl and mix to combine. Serve with kebabs.

Note: When threading the vegetables onto the skewers make sure that the vegetables have a flat outside surface – this will make them easier to grill.

Tahini is a thick oily paste made from crushed toasted sesame seeds. On standing the oil tends to separate out and before using it is necessary to beat it back into the paste. It is available from Middle Eastern food and health food stores and most supermarkets.

Serves 4

ingredients

3 zucchini (courgettes), cut into 2cm/³/₄in cubes
2 red peppers, cut into 2cm/³/₄in cubes
2 yellow or green peppers, cut into 2cm/³/₄in cubes
8 patty pan squash, halved
185 g/6 oz feta cheese, cut into 2cm/³/₄in cubes
2 tablespoons chilli oil

<u>Tahini dip</u>
¹/₂ cup/125g/4oz tahini
3 tablespoons thick natural yoghurt
2 tablespoons lime juice
1 tablespoon sweet chilli sauce
1 tablespoon tomato paste (purée)
freshly ground black pepper

No barbecue book would be complete without a section on the extras that seem to make everyone else's barbecue a raging success. In this chapter you will find many secrets for perfect barbecuing.

Savoury Butters

Savoury butters are a great way to add taste after cooking – place a piece on a steak or in a baked potato. Garlic butter is probably the best known, but you can make a variety of tasty butters.

To make a parsley butter, place 125 g/4 oz softened butter, a dash of lemon juice, 1 tablespoon finely chopped fresh parsley and pepper to taste in a food processor or blender and process to combine. Shape butter into a log, wrap in plastic food wrap and refrigerate until firm.

This is the basic recipe for a savoury butter and the parsley can be replaced with any flavouring of your choice. Any fresh herbs can be used in place of the parsley – you might like to try chives, rosemary, thyme or basil. Combining different herbs can create an interesting flavour. Other delicious flavours are horseradish, anchovy, roasted red or green pepper, curry paste, mustard, onion, spring onions, capers, finely grated lemon or lime rind.

Barbecue sauce

1 tablespoon vegetable oil
1 onion, chopped
1 clove garlic, crushed
1 teaspoon mustard powder
1 tablespoon Worcestershire sauce
1 tablespoon brown sugar
3 tablespoons tomato sauce
1 teaspoon chilli sauce
3/4 cup/185mL/6fl oz beef stock
freshly ground black pepper

Heat oil in a saucepan and cook onion and garlic for 3-4 minutes or until soft. Stir in mustard powder, Worcestershire sauce, sugar, tomato sauce, chilli sauce and stock. Bring to the boil, then reduce heat and simmer for 8-10 minutes or until sauce reduces and thickens slightly. Season to taste with black pepper.

Makes 1 cup/250 mL/8 fl oz

Mexican chilli sauce

Wonderful with steak, chops or sausages, this sauce will spice up any meal.

2 tablespoons vegetable oil
2 small fresh red chillies, seeded and finely chopped
3 small fresh green chillies, seeded and finely chopped
3 cloves garlic, crushed
2 onions, finely chopped
1 tablespoon finely chopped fresh coriander
440g/14oz canned tomatoes, undrained and mashed
1 teaspoon brown sugar

¹/₂ teaspoon ground cinnamon
¹/₄ teaspoon ground cloves
¹/₄ teaspoon ground ginger
2 tablespoons lemon juice
3 tablespoons water

Heat oil in a frying pan and cook red and green chillies, garlic, onions and coriander for 2-3 minutes. Stir in tomatoes, sugar, cinnamon, cloves, ginger, lemon juice and water. Bring to the boil, then reduce heat and simmer for 15-20 minutes or until sauce reduces and thickens.

Makes 2 cups/500 mL/16 fl oz

Sweet and sour barbecue sauce

A sweet and sour sauce is always a popular accompaniment for chicken and pork, but is also delicious served with sausages and fish.

1 tablespoon vegetable oil
1 small onion, chopped
1 red pepper, chopped
1 tablespoon soy sauce
2 tablespoons honey
1 tablespoon tomato paste (purée)
2 tablespoons cornflour
¹/₂ cup/125mL/4fl oz cider vinegar
¹/₂ cup/125mL/4fl oz chicken stock or water
440g/14oz canned pineapple pieces, drained

1 Heat oil in a saucepan and cook onion and red pepper for 4-5 minutes or until soft. Place soy sauce, honey, tomato paste (purée), cornflour and vinegar in a bowl and mix to combine.

2 Stir cornflour mixture into vegetables, then stir in stock or water. Cook, stirring, over a medium heat for 2-3 minutes or until sauce boils and thickens. Stir in pineapple pieces and cook for 2-3 minutes longer.

Makes 2 cups/500 mL/16 fl oz

Apple and horseradish sauce

Delicious served with beef and sausages, this condiment also makes an interesting accompaniment for barbecued fish.

¹/₂ cup/125mL/4fl oz cream (double)
1 green apple, cored and grated
3 tablespoons horseradish relish
freshly ground black pepper

Place cream in a bowl and whip until soft peaks form. Fold in apple and horseradish relish and season to taste with black pepper.

Makes 1 cup/250 mL/8 fl oz

barbecue
secrets

What's in a marinade

A marinade tenderises the tough, moistens the dry and flavours the bland. It can be that secret ingredient that turns an otherwise ordinary piece of meat, fish, poultry or game into a taste sensation.

A marinade consists of an acid ingredient, an oil and flavourings – each ingredient playing an important role in the marinating process.

The acid ingredient:

This can be lemon or lime juice, vinegar, wine, soy sauce, yogurt or tomatoes. The acid in a marinade tenderises foods such as beef, lamb, pork, poultry and seafood.

The oil:

The moisturiser in the marinade. Olive and vegetable oils are the most popular but nut, herb or seed oils can also add an interesting flavour. A rule of thumb is that a marinade for barbecuing or grilling should contain at least 25 per cent oil, so each 1 cup/250mL/8fl oz of marinade, should include 1/4 cup/60mL/2fl oz oil.

The flavourings:

Most commonly these are fresh or dried herbs and spices, garlic, ginger or onions.

How to marinate:

As marinades contain acid ingredients, the food and marinade should be placed in stainless steel, enamel, glass or ceramic dishes. The marinade should come up around the sides of the food, but need not completely cover it. Turn the food several times during marinating. Food can also be marinated in a plastic food bag. This is particularly good for marinating large pieces of meat such as roasts. Place the food and marinade in the bag, squeeze out as much air as possible and seal with a rubber band or tie with a piece of string. Turn the bag several times during marinating.

How long to marinate:

Marinating times can be anywhere between 15 minutes and 2 days. As a general rule, the longer you marinate the more tender and flavoursome the food will be. Food marinates faster at room temperature than in the refrigerator. But remember, in hot weather it is usually better to allow a longer marinating time in the refrigerator to ensure that the food stays safe to eat. Fish and seafood should not be marinated for longer than 30 minutes, as the acid ingredient in the marinade will 'cook' the fish. If marinating in the refrigerator, allow the food to stand at room temperature for 30 minutes before cooking to ensure even cooking of the marinated food.

Cooking marinated food:

Drain the food well before cooking, especially when cooking in a frying pan or on a barbecue plate (griddle). Wet food will stew rather than brown. The remaining marinade can be brushed over the food several times during cooking.

Coffee honey marinade

This delicious no-salt-added marinade is excellent for beef and lamb.

1 tablespoon honey
1 tablespoon instant coffee powder
1/4 cup/60 mL/2 fl oz lemon juice
2 cloves garlic, crushed

1 Place honey, coffee powder, lemon juice and garlic in a small bowl and mix to combine.
2 Pour marinade over meat, cover and set aside to marinate.

White wine and herb marinade

This tasty marinade is ideal for fish and poultry. Choose the herbs that you like or that are in season.

³/₄ **cup/185 mL/6fl oz white wine**
¹/₄ **cup/60 mL/2 fl oz olive oil**
2 spring onions, finely chopped
I tablespoon chopped fresh herbs, or
I teaspoon dried herbs

1 *Place wine, oil, spring onions and herbs in a bowl and mix to combine.*
2 *Pour marinade over poultry or fish, cover and set aside to marinate.*

Red wine marinade

An excellent marinade for any type of red meat or game. For lighter meat, such as lamb, choose a lighter red wine – for example a Pinot Noir – while for game you can use a heavier red wine such as a Hermitage.

I¹/₂ **cups/375mL/12fl oz red wine**
¹/₂ **cup/125mL/4fl oz olive oil**
I small onion, diced
I bay leaf, torn into pieces
I teaspoon black peppercorns, cracked
I clove garlic, crushed
3 teaspoons finely chopped fresh thyme or I teaspoon dried thyme

1 *Place wine, oil, onion, bay leaf, peppercorns, garlic and thyme in a small bowl and mix to combine.*
2 *Pour marinade over meat, cover and set aside to marinate.*

Lemon herb marinade

¹/₂ **cup/125 mL/4fl oz olive oil**
¹/₄ **cup/60 mL/2fl oz lemon juice**
¹/₄ **cup/60 mL/2fl oz white wine vinegar**
I clove garlic, crushed
I teaspoon finely grated lemon rind
2 teaspoons finely chopped fresh parsley
2 teaspoons snipped fresh chives

3 teaspoons finely chopped fresh rosemary or I teaspoon finely chopped dried rosemary

1 *Place oil, lemon juice, vinegar, garlic, lemon rind, parsley, chives and rosemary in a small bowl and mix to combine.*
2 *Pour marinade over meat or poultry, cover and set aside to marinate.*

Hot chilli marinade

¹/₄ **cup/60 mL/2fl oz soy sauce**
¹/₄ **cup/60 mL/2fl oz hoisin sauce**
¹/₂ **cup/125 mL/4fl oz dry sherry**
I clove garlic, crushed
I teaspoon grated fresh ginger
2 spring onions, finely chopped
I teaspoon hot chilli sauce

1 *Place soy sauce, hoisin sauce, sherry, garlic, ginger, spring onions and chilli sauce in a small bowl and mix to combine.*
2 *Pour marinade over meat or poultry, cover and set aside to marinate. Use the marinade as a baste when barbecuing.*

Cooking is not an exact science: one does not require finely calibrated scales, pipettes and scientific equipment to cook, yet the conversion to metric measures in some countries and its interpretations must have intimidated many a good cook.

Weights are given in the recipes only for ingredients such as meats, fish, poultry and some vegetables. Though a few grams/ounces one way or another will not affect the success of your dish.

Though recipes have been tested using the Australian Standard 250mL cup, 20mL tablespoon and 5mL teaspoon, they will work just as well with the US and Canadian 8fl oz cup, or the UK 300mL cup. We have used graduated cup measures in preference to tablespoon measures so that proportions are always the same. Where tablespoon measures have been given, these are not crucial measures, so using the smaller tablespoon of the US or UK will not affect the recipe's success. At least we all agree on the teaspoon size.

For breads, cakes and pastries, the only area which might cause concern is where eggs are used, as proportions will then vary. If working with a 250mL or 300mL cup, use large eggs (60g/2oz), adding a little more liquid to the recipe for 300mL cup measures if it seems necessary. Use the medium-sized eggs (55g/1¹/₄oz) with 8fl oz cup measure. A graduated set of measuring cups and spoons is recommended, the cups in particular for measuring dry ingredients. Remember to level such ingredients to ensure their accuracy.

English measures

All measurements are similar to Australian with two exceptions: the English cup measures 300mL/10fl oz, whereas the Australian cup measure 250mL/8fl oz. The English tablespoon (the Australian dessertspoon) measures 14.8mL/¹/₂fl oz against the Australian tablespoon of 20mL/³/₄fl oz.

American measures

The American reputed pint is 16fl oz, a quart is equal to 32fl oz and the American gallon, 128fl oz. The Imperial measurement is 20fl oz to the pint, 40fl oz a quart and 160fl oz one gallon.

The American tablespoon is equal to 14.8mL/¹/₂fl oz, the teaspoon is 5mL/¹/₆fl oz. The cup measure is 250mL/8fl oz, the same as Australia.

Dry measures

All the measures are level, so when you have filled a cup or spoon, level it off with the edge of a knife. The scale below is the "cook's equivalent"; it is not an exact conversion of metric to imperial measurement. To calculate the exact metric equivalent yourself, use 2.2046 lb = 1kg or 1 lb = 0.45359kg

Metric		Imperial	
g = grams		oz = ounces	
kg = kilograms		lb = pound	
15g		¹/₂oz	
20g		²/₃oz	
30g		1oz	
60g		2oz	
90g		3oz	
125g		4oz	¹/₄ lb
155g		5oz	
185g		6oz	
220g		7oz	
250g		8oz	¹/₂ lb
280g		9oz	
315g		10oz	
345g		11oz	
375g		12oz	³/₄ lb
410g		13oz	
440g		14oz	
470g		15oz	
1,000g	1kg	35.2oz	2.2 lb
	1.5kg		3.3 lb

Oven temperatures

The Celsius temperatures given here are not exact; they have been rounded off and are given as a guide only. Follow the manufacturer's temperature guide, relating it to oven description given in the recipe. Remember gas ovens are hottest at the top, electric ovens at the bottom and convection-fan forced ovens are usually even throughout. We included Regulo numbers for gas cookers which may assist. To convert °C to °F multiply °C by 9 and divide by 5 then add 32.

Oven temperatures

	C°	F°	Regulo
Very slow	120	250	1
Slow	150	300	2
Moderately slow	150	325	3
Moderate	180	350	4
Moderately hot	190-200	370-400	5-6
Hot	210-220	410-440	6-7
Very hot	230	450	8
Super hot	250-290	475-500	9-10

Cake dish sizes

Metric	Imperial
15cm	6in
18cm	7in
20cm	8in
23cm	9in

Loaf dish sizes

Metric	Imperial
23x12cm	9x5in
25x8cm	10x3in
28x18cm	11x7in

Liquid measures

Metric	Imperial	Cup & Spoon
mL	fl oz	
millilitres	fluid ounce	
5mL	$^1/_6$fl oz	1 teaspoon
20mL	$^2/_3$fl oz	1 tablespoon
30mL	1fl oz	1 tablespoon plus 2 teaspoons
60mL	2fl oz	$^1/_4$ cup
85mL	2$^1/_2$fl oz	$^1/_3$ cup
100mL	3fl oz	$^3/_8$ cup
125mL	4fl oz	$^1/_2$ cup
150mL	5fl oz	$^1/_4$ pint, 1 gill
250mL	8fl oz	1 cup
300mL	10fl oz	$^1/_2$ pint)
360mL	12fl oz	1$^1/_2$ cups
420mL	14fl oz	1$^3/_4$ cups
500mL	16fl oz	2 cups
600mL	20fl oz 1 pint,	2$^1/_2$ cups
1 litre	35fl oz 1$^3/_4$ pints,	4 cups

Cup measurements

One cup is equal to the following weights.

	Metric	Imperial
Almonds, flaked	90g	3oz
Almonds, slivered, ground	125g	4oz
Almonds, kernel	155g	5oz
Apples, dried, chopped	125g	4oz
Apricots, dried, chopped	190g	6oz
Breadcrumbs, packet	125g	4oz

	Metric	Imperial
Breadcrumbs, soft	60g	2oz
Cheese, grated	125g	4oz
Choc bits	155g	5oz
Coconut, desiccated	90g	3oz
Cornflakes	30g	1oz
Currants	155g	5oz
Flour	125g	4oz
Fruit, dried (mixed, sultanas etc)	185g	6oz
Ginger, crystallised, glace	250g	8oz
Honey, treacle, golden syrup	315g	10oz
Mixed peel	220g	7oz
Nuts, chopped	125g	4oz
Prunes, chopped	220g	7oz
Rice, cooked	155g	5oz
Rice, uncooked	220g	7oz
Rolled oats	90g	3oz
Sesame seeds	125g	4oz
Shortening (butter, margarine)	250g	8oz
Sugar, brown	155g	5oz
Sugar, granulated or caster	250g	8oz
Sugar, sifted icing	155g	5oz
Wheatgerm	60g	2oz

Length

Some of us still have trouble converting imperial length to metric. In this scale, measures have been rounded off to the easiest-to-use and most acceptable figures.

To obtain the exact metric equivalent in converting inches to centimetres, multiply inches by 2.54 whereby 1 inch equals 25.4 millimetres and 1 millimetre equals 0.03937 inches.

Metric	Imperial
mm=millimetres	in = inches
cm=centimetres	ft = feet
5mm, 0.5cm	$^1/_4$in
10mm, 1.0cm	$^1/_2$in
20mm, 2.0cm	$^3/_4$in
2.5cm	1in
5cm	2in
8cm	3in
10cm	4in
12cm	5in
15cm	6in
18cm	7in
20cm	8in
23cm	9in
25cm	10in
28cm	11in
30cm	1 ft, 12in

index